GOOD
HOUSEKEEPING
Book of
Wholefood Cookery

GOOD HOUSEKEEPING

Book of
Wholefood Cookery

Text by
Gail Duff

with recipes supplied by the
Good Housekeeping Institute

EBURY PRESS
LONDON

Published by Ebury Press
National Magazine House
72 Broadwick Street
London W1V 2BP

First impression 1980

ISBN 0 85223 180 6

Editor Helen Southall
Designer Harry Green
Senior home economist Susanna Tee
Assistant home economists Marion Budden, Jenny Slack
Line drawings by Vanessa Luff
Colour photography by Melvin Grey, pages 34, 51, 87, 88, 106,
123, 142, 195, 196, 213, 214, 231, 232; Philip Dowell, pages 33 and 177;
Paul Kemp, pages 52, 69, 141; Bryce Attwell, pages 70, 159, 160;
Barry Bullough, pages 105 and 178; and Stephen Baker, page 124.

The publishers would like to thank the
Craftsmen Potters Association of Great Britain for
their help in providing props for photography.

Note When using the recipes in this book, follow either the
metric or imperial measures as they are not interchangeable.

Filmset in Great Britain by
Advanced Filmsetters (Glasgow) Ltd.
Printed and bound by
New Interlitho s.p.a., Milan

Contents

An Introduction to Wholefoods

Wholefoods have certainly been talked about a good deal recently, and there have been some very conflicting views expressed through the media about what we should and should not eat, but there is still some confusion as to exactly what wholefoods are. This talk about our eating habits, although baffling at times, has served one very good purpose: it has made many wives and mothers wake up to the fact that there is more to feeding the family than simply satisfying their immediate hunger with convenience and processed foods. They are thinking, perhaps for the first time, about which foods will help make their children, their husbands and themselves fit and healthy.

It is very difficult to develop a new approach to eating, especially if you are not quite certain which foods you should or should not be buying, so let us begin by looking at what wholefoods really are. You will probably find that they are not all as unfamiliar or strange as you have been led to believe.

The dictionary says that if something is whole, it is complete, with nothing added and nothing taken away. Whole can also mean undamaged; and another meaning, perhaps a little old-fashioned now but very relevant here, is healthy. If you apply all these to food, you are left with good, basic ingredients that have been grown or produced by natural means, coming to you fresh, sound and undamaged and as close as possible to their original state. None of their basic constituents should have been taken away and nothing else should have been added by way of chemicals, colourings or preservatives.

If your first thought is 'How can I possibly apply that to everything I buy?' just think how often the description can apply to the items of food that you already buy every week. Fresh fruit and vegetables are the obvious example. What could be more whole than these? Then there are eggs and dairy products, fresh meat and fish. All these can be found in every household. Wholemeal flour, bread and pasta are becoming increasingly popular. So is brown rice, and you probably have some dried beans or lentils in the store-cupboard. All these ingredients are used in everyday cooking, but can still be called wholefood.

So you see, to be a wholefood family, you will not have to live on tons of grains and carrot juice. You will have plenty of ingredients to choose from and the structure of your meals need not change at all; although in some cases lighter cooking methods will be called for.

You don't have to be a vegetarian either. Both vegetarians and meat eaters can eat wholefoods. The basic constituents of their diets, apart from meat, can be exactly the same and the two groups can be equally healthy.

Wholefood eating is not just an upper-class fad. It should be, and is, available to anyone who wants to try it. Wholefood shops are becoming the norm in local high streets and shopping centres and even supermarkets are more aware of the public demand for this type of food; so you should have no trouble in finding your ingredients. And once you have stocked your store-cupboard you should find that wholefood eating is not costing you any more money; in fact it might even prove cheaper.

Wholefoods are not medicine and should not be treated as such. Even if you are changing to them for health reasons, you will come to find that not only do they do you good, they also taste exceptionally good; and so could easily turn you and your family into healthy gourmets.

Why eat wholefoods?

Our grandparents never even thought about wholefoods and they were healthy enough, so why is there suddenly so much concern about the food we should and should not eat? The answer is that our grandparents did not have to worry, since the basic average diet in their day was more natural than ours is today. Throughout this century the Western diet has become softer, sweeter and richer in fats and we have come to rely as much on the food technologist, with his chemicals and various means of preservation, as we do on

the farmer and grower. As a result, although medical care has become more sophisticated, there has been an alarming increase in what have come to be called the Western diseases of affluence. These include heart disease, obesity, diabetes, gallstones, dental decay, appendicitis, diverticulosis, varicose veins, piles, deep vein thrombosis and colonic cancer. It is a formidable list and it is becoming more and more evident that all these diseases are linked with the way we eat. Would it not be better, instead of doing a patching-up job once the disease has developed, to take out an 'insurance policy' against these diseases occurring by way of healthy and sensible eating patterns? The diseases may not be prevented altogether, but they will certainly become less frequent and severe.

Apart from those people who suffer from specific complaints, there are few who can say they feel 100% fit, even for part of the time. A recent survey showed that 60–80% fitness was more likely to be the average figure which, when you think about it, isn't all that good. If we all increased the percentage by only 10, just think how much better we would feel. A sound, healthy diet can go a long way towards ridding you of minor health problems such as a constant winter sniffle or an unclear skin. It will also help to make you feel more vital and energetic, and 'off days' will become less frequent.

If beauty and looks are your concern then you have only to read about what the top models are eating these days to realise that wholefood can play a large part here, too. Wholefood helps towards a fresh complexion and healthy hair and helps you maintain a slim figure. If you are overweight and start to eat wholefoods, you may find that you lose a few pounds without even trying. If not, then you will certainly find it easier to slim than on a diet of refined and processed foods. Wholemeal bread, for example, is bulkier and more satisfying than white, cooking methods require less fat and you can stave off between-meals' hunger pangs with fresh, crisp salads or fruit instead of snacks.

It is not only children who need food to build up their body tissues. Our bodies continue to change and replace themselves all through our lives and in order for this to happen we need food which our systems can break down and utilise. We must think whether we would rather use wholesome and natural building materials or whether we want to be made from manufacturers' chemicals and devitalised processed foods. The

old comparison of our bodies being like cars that need fuel for energy is a very good one. We want to put first class petrol and pure oil into our cars to give them a long and trouble-free life. Surely our bodies deserve the same respect?

It is no good thinking that if you change to wholefoods, all your ills will disappear within a week. The effect of food on the body is a very gradual process which can be seen by the fact that the body takes seven years to replace itself completely. But after a few months you will start to find that your insurance policy is beginning to pay off.

Balancing the diet

Even without the manufactured and the processed, there is such a wide range of foods available and such a variety of combinations and cooking methods, that a wholefood diet need never be boring.

Eating a varied selection of food every day is good for us in another way as well. In order to be healthy and work well, our bodies need at least forty different nutrients, all of which are supplied by the food we eat. The quantities of these substances that we need vary considerably. In some cases we may need only a tiny amount, but a lack of any one of them can lead to ill health. Different types of food contain different nutrients and so the more mixed and varied our diet, the more likely it is that we will obtain every essential one.

A well-balanced meal, containing as many nutrients as possible, is what we should aim for and is not difficult to achieve. Even if you don't eat wholefoods regularly and have never given a thought to things like proteins and carbohydrates, you will probably be balancing most of your meals automatically from common sense, recognising the different qualities of the different ingredients you buy. For the main meal, the traditional 'meat and two veg' is the obvious example. The meat will provide us with proteins and fats, potatoes with carbohydrates, and a green vegetable with additional vitamins and minerals not supplied by the other two. You probably would never serve just two kinds of meat, or potatoes with dumplings, or several types of green vegetables and nothing else. Even snack meals can be balanced. An extreme example of an

unbalanced snack is a 'chip butty', providing mainly carbohydrates and fats; but wholemeal bread with cheese and a tomato would give you a variety of different nutrients, besides contrasting tastes, flavours and textures for you to enjoy.

Any diet, even if it is a low calorie one designed to help you slim, must contain certain amounts of proteins, carbohydrates and fats. You cannot cut one out of the diet altogether and remain healthy.

PROTEINS We need proteins for growth when we are young, and all through our lives they are essential for the maintenance and repair of our body tissues, for firm muscle tone and for healthy hair, skin and blood. Although we tend to think only of the animal products like meat, fish, eggs and dairy produce as the ones which contain proteins, there are many other foods which help to supply our daily requirements.

Proteins are made up of substances called amino acids which structurally exist in chains. The amino acid chains in animal products are very similar to the ones which exist in our own bodies, and as such we can eat them alone and obtain the kind of protein that we require, ie 'first class' proteins. There are, however, other protein foods: pulses, nuts and seeds, whole grains and some fresh vegetables. The protein chains in any one of these are deficient in one or more of the essential amino acids; but if they are eaten together the amino acids will combine to make complete chains. In this way, the secondary protein foods can be just as nourishing as animal proteins. Remember, though, that the body does not store amino acids so it is important to combine as many as possible together in one meal. Beans on wholemeal toast with a green salad containing a few nuts is a good example.

CARBOHYDRATES Carbohydrates provide the body with energy and are obtained from sugars and starches. In a wholefood diet, the most healthy foods which provide them are whole grains, vegetables and fruits. These also provide other nutrients and fibre which, together with the starch, satisfy us far longer than something sweet and sugary which will give us a quick burst of energy for a short time and will not satisfy our hunger pangs easily. This leads to us eating far more than we should and to the excess being stored by our bodies as fat.

FATS There has been more talk about fats than anything else of late and probably more confusion. Firstly, we must realise that whatever we think of fats, we cannot give them up altogether. They are absolutely essential to our health as they carry fat-soluble vitamins (A, D, E and K) round the body, protect our tissues, organs and nerves and help to maintain an even body temperature.

Dietary fats do not only consist of the various oils, butter and margarines with which we cook and the visible fat on meat. There are also invisible fats within the structure of all animal products and oily fish, and in nuts, seeds and soya beans.

VITAMINS AND MINERALS Both vitamins and minerals are found in foods in very small amounts, but a lack of any one of them could be seriously damaging. For example, no vitamin C in the diet can eventually cause scurvy and lack of calcium in children leads to retarded development of bones. Much research is still being done in this field and new substances and functions are still being discovered. If you are careful about balancing your diet and eat a variety of wholefoods, you should have no problems in obtaining the right proportions of vitamins and minerals and, although some wholefood shops carry a wide range of vitamin pills and dietary supplements, if you are fit and healthy, you should not really need them.

The charts below show the most well-known vitamins and minerals. There are others, but their functions and sources are not so easily defined.

Vitamin	Needed for	Sources
A (retinol)	Growth, healthy eyes and skin	Yellow fruit, green vegetables and carrots, oily fish, fish liver oils, dairy foods, eggs, liver, heart, kidney, butter, margarine
B_1 (thiamin)	Growth, conversion of carbohydrates to energy, muscle and nerve health	Whole grain foods, yeast, meat, soya beans, potatoes
B_2 (riboflavin)	Utilisation of energy from food, growth, healthy skin, eyes and mouth	Milk, whole grain foods, yeast, meat, soya beans, eggs, potatoes
pantothenic acid (B group)	Release of energy from fat and carbohydrate, tissue growth, healthy skin, growth and health of hair	Whole grains, yeast, liver, eggs
B_6 (pyridoxine)	Healthy skin, nerves and muscle, protein metabolism	Whole grains, meat, fish, milk, yeast, some vegetables
B_{12} (cobalamins or cyanocobalamin)	Healthy blood, growth, protein metabolism, healthy nerves and skin	Liver, meat, eggs, milk, cheese
biotin (B group)	Fat metabolism, healthy skin, muscles, nerves	Liver, kidney, egg yolk, dairy products
choline and inositol (B group)	Healthy liver, preventing build-up of fats	Liver, kidneys, eggs, yeast
folic acid (B group)	Growth, healthy blood	Liver, kidneys, green vegetables, yeast, pulses, oranges
nicotinic acid (niacin) (B group)	Utilisation of food energy, healthy skin and nerves, growth	Meat, milk, bread, fish
C (ascorbic acid)	Healthy gums and teeth, blood vessels and cells, healing process, resistance to infection, absorption of iron	Fruit and vegetables
D (calciferol)	Formation of bones and teeth, metabolism of calcium and phosphorus	Oily fish, fish liver oils, eggs, butter and margarine, sunshine on skin
E (tocopherol)	Thought to be essential for fertility and muscle health	Whole grains, vegetable oils, nuts, eggs
K	Blood clotting	Green vegetables, pith of citrus fruits, liver, soya beans, oils

Mineral	Needed for	Sources
calcium	Strength, healthy bones, nerves, kidneys and muscles, blood clotting	Milk and dairy products, green vegetables, bread, nuts and seeds
iodine	Hormone balance	White fish and shellfish
iron	Healthy blood, utilisation of oxygen, resistance to fatigue	Liver, meat, whole grains, dried apricots, molasses
magnesium	Utilisation of energy, healthy nerves and heart	Whole grains, vegetables
potassium	Healthy kidneys, steady blood pressure	Vegetables, meat, milk

The Question of Refinement

Since medieval times it has been thought that white is beautiful and white bread and sugar served at the table were symbols of a wealthy household. Now, at last, we are beginning to realise where we have been going wrong. In refining products and making them white, we take out vitamins, minerals and fibre, leaving a commodity very high in concentrated starch and calories, with no bulk or goodness.

Refined foods tend to be soft and you do not notice them too much when you eat them. For example, it takes 2.7 kg (6 lb) sugar beet to make 450 g (1 lb) refined sugar. It takes very little time to eat a small amount of sugar, but how much longer you would need to eat the equivalent in its natural form. You would probably give up long before you had chewed your way through all that sugar beet and yet your energy requirement would still be satisfied.

If we feel hungry and eat, for example, a chocolate bar or a slice of white bread, the energy supplied is quickly absorbed and stored by our bodies. Within an hour, we are hungry again, repeat the process and therefore become fat. If we eat unrefined foods, such as raw fruits, instead of chocolate, wholemeal bread instead of white, they will take longer to chew, they will be more bulky in the stomach and the energy they give will be absorbed very slowly. We will therefore be more satisfied for a longer time and have the added benefit of the extra fibre and vitamins.

It is lack of fibre that is now thought to be the cause of many of our Western diseases, particularly those of the digestive system. A high fibre diet with plenty of fruit, vegetables and whole grains will help the passage of food and waste products through our bodies, thus ridding us of any previous discomfort. It has also been shown that fibre can slightly reduce the absorption of calories from fats, aiding the war against inches.

Flour

One of the products that suffers most from refinement is flour. All types of flour have the same beginning: a whole grain of wheat. And although it is very tiny, its make-up is quite complex.

A wheat grain consists basically of three parts: the outer coating which we call the bran, taking up 8% of the grain; the tiny growing point called the germ, which accounts for 2%; and the large, white centre called the endosperm, consisting mostly of starch and taking up the final 90%. The bran provides us with essential fibre and the germ contains protein, vitamin E, most of the vitamins of the B group and many valuable minerals.

100% WHOLEMEAL FLOUR (ALSO CALLED 100% WHOLEWHEAT) When the whole of the wheat grain is ground up into flour the result is 100% wholemeal (or wholewheat) flour, containing all the endosperm, bran and germ and therefore all the essential fibre and nutrients in the right proportions. This flour is the best and healthiest the wholefood cook can use and with it you can make bread, scones, pastry, cakes and biscuits. You can use it in sauces and soups and as a coating for meat and fish; in fact in any way that you use white flour. Most of the flour in Britain is roller ground on large metal rollers, but some wholemeal and wheatmeal (see below) flours are stone ground in the traditional way. This makes very little difference nutritionally and the wholefood cook can use either stone or roller ground flour. Both plain and self raising types of wholemeal flour are readily available.

81% AND 84% WHEATMEAL FLOURS If you want a finer flour, for a special cake for example, but still want one that is full of goodness, then choose a flour of 81% or 84% extraction. This means that all the bran has been removed but the germ, together with all its vitamins, minerals and protein, has been maintained. The flour is fine and a pale biscuit colour and is available in both plain and self raising forms.

GRANARY FLOUR This is a plain flour made from 81% or 84% wheatmeal flour with whole, malted grains of wheat and rye mixed in. Bread and scones made from it have a delicious, nutty flavour and a coarse texture. They also rise well because the flour has a high gluten content. Granary flour is best used as an occasional change since it has not the bran content of 100% wholemeal flours.

WHITE FLOURS When all the bran and germ are removed from the crushed wheat grain you get white flour, which is a 70% extraction and consists of the starchy endosperm only. It has very little goodness left in it so, by law, certain substances must be replaced artificially. One substance added is powdered chalk which has no proven nutritive value. Iron is added, but not in a form that we can easily absorb. The other compulsory additives are two of the B vitamins but their eventual effect is doubtful since all the B vitamins work together and simply adding two upsets the balance. It is the lack of fibre in white bread that is causing most concern at the moment. There is a certain amount, but to obtain your recommended daily intake you would have to eat 3.4 kg ($7\frac{1}{2}$ lb) white bread compared with 150 g (5 oz) 100% wholemeal.

When white flour is freshly ground it is not actually white but a pale cream colour. This is known as unbleached flour and is available in plain and self raising varieties. This flour still contains a small proportion of vitamin E and wheatgerm oil. After a few months' storage the oil may go rancid. Therefore, to improve the shelf-life of the flour and also to make it the pure white that bakers and some housewives prefer, it is

bleached in a sealed gas chamber with a dangerous substance called chlorine dioxide. None of this substance is left in the flour by the end of the process, but there is no vitamin E either.

Strong white flours may be bleached or unbleached. They are a 70% extraction of hard, imported wheats which are more suitable for breadmaking than those grown in this country. None of the white flours, whether ordinary, unbleached or strong, are used in wholefood cookery.

Other wheat products

Although the wholefood cook does not use refined flours, she can take advantage of the products of refining. In the wholefood shop and, increasingly, in the supermarket, you will find packets of bran and wheatgerm. Use these to enrich your home-made bread and cakes, sprinkle them over gratin dishes, cereals and soufflés, use them as a coating and to make crumble toppings. They will always add extra goodness to any dish.

Bread

If you become enthusiastic about wholefood cooking, you will most likely want to make your own bread, but until you find your feet, you may find it best to buy it. In this case, always make sure that what you are buying really is wholemeal as assistants in the bakers can be as confused about wholemeal, wheatmeal and brown as the customer.

Breads made with 100% wholemeal flour are called wholemeal or wholewheat. Those made with 81% or 84% flour or with a mixture of white flour and 100% wholemeal flour are called wheatmeal. Breads just called 'brown' may be wheatmeal, but are more likely to be made from coloured white flour. Wheatgerm breads are generally made from a wheatmeal or lower extraction flour with added wheatgerm. Bran enriched breads can be made in the same way, or they can simply be made with white flour and added bran. 100% wholemeal (or wholewheat) bread is what the wholefood shopper should be buying.

Sugar

We have always had a sweet tooth but never, it seems, more than now. Every year the consumption of sugar per head in this country is almost 54.4 kg (120 lb). In a wholefood diet, however, you will come to use extremely less, and instead of white sugars you will be using natural brown sugars like Barbados and demerara.

It is always easier to stop using a certain food if you know the reasons why you should, so let's first look at the bad news about white sugar and then see what we can replace it with.

White sugars are refined from sugar cane and, increasingly, sugar beet. Juice is pressed from them which then goes through a long process of evaporation and crystallisation to produce, in the end, a product which is 99% sucrose, all the other original nutrients of the beet or cane having been taken away.

On average, a quarter of our calorie intake is supplied by sugar, but these are so-called 'empty calories', bringing with them no vitamins, minerals or fibre. It is easy to consume too many and we recognise the fact when our clothes no longer fit. Because sugar gives us quick bursts of energy instead of a steady supply, our moods, as well as our ability to work, are constantly going up and down. Although sugar is never listed as an addictive drug, the more we have, the more we tend to want.

In order to digest sugar, various other substances have to be called upon. One of these is thiamin (vitamin B_1). Digesting sugar uses it up quickly, whereas if we ate other carbohydrate foods that contained it (wholemeal bread and vegetables) there would be no danger of deficiency at all. Insulin, produced by the pancreas, is also needed in the digestion of sugar.

Last, but certainly not least, sugar has been proved to be one of the major causes of tooth decay. Wouldn't it be lovely to go for our regular dental check-up with confidence, knowing that the dentist will find little to do?

However, a wholefood way of life does not mean that you have to be completely spartan and give up sugar altogether. A little sweet food occasionally will do no harm; and there are some sugars that are certainly better for you than the refined white ones.

As with bread, you do have to make sure that you are buying the right kinds. There are various steps in the refining process of sugar that produce sweet substances; and the lower down the process you go the more vitamins and minerals this will contain.

DEMERARA SUGAR One step down from white sugar is demerara, so called because it came originally from Demerara County in Guyana. It consists of large, golden crystals, which are usually slightly sticky, and contains a few B vitamins (but not thiamin) and some minerals. Genuine demerara will have its country of origin on the packet and nothing else. Beware of the manufactured variety, sometimes called London demerara, which is made from refined white sugar with a thin coating of molasses. If you look, this will be stated on the packet.

BARBADOS SUGAR Next in line come Barbados or Muscovado sugars which are often referred to as raw sugars. You can buy light and dark varieties, and they are both very soft and sticky and finely grained. Both contain B vitamins (including thiamin) which help to digest them and small amounts of minerals including calcium and potassium.

Here again, there is a refined counterpart, generally referred to as soft brown sugar, which is made from fine grain white sugar and sugar syrups. To be sure you are buying the right commodity, always look at the pack. A list of ingredients means that it is not genuine.

MOLASSES SUGAR The raw sugar which contains the most goodness is molasses sugar, which is the least refined and very dark and sticky. It is also called Black Barbados or demerara molasses. It has a very strong molasses flavour and is best used in baking.

Other sweeteners

MOLASSES Thick, dark, syrupy molasses is the first substance produced by the process of refining sugar cane. It contains ten different minerals, a large amount of B vitamins and about two thirds the calories of white sugar. It has a fairly strong flavour and you will need a far smaller amount of molasses than sugar in any recipe.

BLACK TREACLE This contains some minerals and B vitamins, but not as many as molasses. The flavour is very similar but most wholefood cooks prefer to use molasses.

GOLDEN SYRUP This is white sugar that has been melted and treated so that it stays syrupy and does not re-crystallise. It has no significant nutritional value and is not considered a wholefood product.

HONEY Honey consists of 75% sugars (mainly in the form of fructose), 20% water and the rest is made up of vitamins A, C, and those of the B group; the mineral chromium which plays a part in the digestion of carbohydrates; and a substance called acetylcholine which helps to maintain a healthy blood pressure. The energy provided by honey is quickly available to the body, although it lasts longer than energy from white sugar. 25 g (1 oz) of honey provides only 80 calories compared with the 112 calories from white sugar.

Honey has also been credited with healing and antiseptic properties. It is probably not the wonder food which some people claim it to be, but it is definitely far better for you than white sugar, and as it tastes richer and sweeter, you will not need so much.

MAPLE SYRUP This is produced by tapping the sap of North American maple trees in early spring and then reducing it quite considerably: 227.5 litres (50 gallons) of sap make 4.5 litres (1 gallon) of syrup. There is a high proportion of sugar in maple syrup, but it is also a good source of the minerals calcium, phosphorus, potassium and sodium. Its rich flavour again means you need far less than you would sugar. Maple syrup is rapidly becoming more popular in Britain and can be bought in 450-g (1-lb) jars like honey. It is a dark, reddish-brown and more liquid than honey, and once the jar is opened it is best kept in the refrigerator.

MALT EXTRACT This is a thick, sticky brown syrup which is produced from germinated and roasted barley grains. It contains protein, B vitamins and minerals and its sugar content consists of maltose which is digested at a much slower rate than sucrose, so giving a constant supply of energy instead of a sudden burst. It is used mainly in baking.

ARTIFICIAL SWEETENERS These are man-made and chemical. Those designed for slimmers provide five hundred times the sweetness of sucrose but no calories. Only one (saccharin and its derivatives) is used now. It has no food value at all and, although research is by no means complete, it is suspected of having the same ill-effects as cyclamates, which were banned in America in 1969.

The other type of artificial sweetener, sorbitol, is made from glucose and so supplies calories. No artificial sweeteners can be considered as wholefood.

Concerning
Fats and Oils

There are basically three types of fats: saturated, monounsaturated and poly-unsaturated; and most fat-containing foods contain a mixture of these in varying proportions.

SATURATED FATS Animal products – meat, butter, lard, hard margarine, cheese and egg yolks – are highest in saturated fats and it is these that have had the finger pointed at them recently in connection with heart disease, since they are thought to raise the levels of cholesterol in the blood. This is the substance which eventually builds up in the arteries causing a blockage and possibly a heart attack.

However, even if we gave up eating anything containing saturated fats the body would still manufacture its own cholesterol since it is necessary for the health and maintenance of our glands, for obtaining vitamin D from sunlight, for lubricating the arteries and for combining with a substance called lecithin to make bile salts which actually help to digest fats. Although cholesterol does build up in the arteries of some people, it has not been proved that it is the cholesterol the person has actually consumed. Some people, for example, can eat large quantities of animal fats and show no trace of heart disease. Others eat small amounts but are nevertheless vulnerable. The facts are probably far more complex than have yet been discovered, the build-up being due to a number of dietary factors such as increased intake of refined foods and additives and a lack of fresh vegetables, besides the eating of too many fats. Other aspects of our life-style such as smoking and lack of exercise might also play a part.

In a wholefood diet, it is best to be careful about eating too many animal fats but there is no need to be fanatical about it. A proportion of lean meat and a little butter, when combined with wholemeal products, fresh fruit and vegetables and alternative forms of protein, will do no harm at all.

POLYUNSATURATED FATS The polyunsaturated fats are those that have been found to reduce the levels of cholesterol in the blood. They are highest in oily fish and the livers of white fish, in nuts, soya beans and vegetable oils.

MONOUNSATURATED FATS Monounsaturated fats are neutral. They neither contribute to the amount of cholesterol in the blood nor reduce it. The oil with the highest proportion of monounsaturated fats is olive oil.

Fat is extremely high in calories and so, in a wholefood diet, it is best to try to cut down all round rather than to banish particular types of fat from the larder.

Fats for cooking, spreading and salads

BUTTER Although it is an animal product containing saturated fats, butter is one of the most natural fats we have. It is made only from churned cream and no chemicals are used in the process at all. Used in moderation, for spreading and cooking, butter will do you no harm and it certainly has a better flavour than margarine.

MARGARINE Margarine is a highly processed fat, but since it was first introduced about a hundred years ago as a cheap substitute for butter, it has been improved upon considerably and there are various types available.

All margarines are 80% fat and no more than 10% of the total fat is allowed to be butter fat. The other fats can be lard or beef tallow, a fish oil such as herring or sardine, any of the vegetable oils, or a mixture.

If, on the label of a margarine, you see 'edible oils' the margarine probably contains a mixture of animal and vegetable oils. Generally, the harder the margarine, the more saturated fats it contains. It need not necessarily contain animal fats, but vegetable fats which have been artificially saturated.

Margarines with a high proportion of polyunsaturated fats are very soft and will not harden even if put in the refrigerator.

About 1.5% of margarine consists of whey solids; there is 2% salt and up to 16% water. The rest is made up of lecithin which is added to stop the margarine spattering when you cook with it; emulsifiers which make the oils mix with the water content (these can be of chemical or natural origin); colouring; flavouring; and vitamins A and D which must be added by law.

When margarines are said to be made from only 'natural ingredients', it does not necessarily mean that they contain no animal products, but that the emulsifiers, colours and flavours are all from natural sources.

From the wholefood point of view, the best margarines to use are the soft types made from natural vegetable ingredients.

LOW FAT SPREADS These are made from similar ingredients to margarine only they have a higher water content in proportion to the amount of fat. They are mainly designed for spreading, but can be used for coating vegetables and for shallow frying. Again, they are a processed product and not really wholefood.

DRIPPING If you are roasting a joint of good quality meat and catch the fat there is no reason why you should not use this dripping occasionally for cooking. It is best not to use bought dripping as it contains preservatives.

LARD You can make your own lard by rendering down pork fat and clarifying it. If you buy lard, look out for the new soft types which do not contain preservatives. These can safely be used in wholefood cooking. Those containing anti-oxidants should really be avoided.

WHITE FATS OR SHORTENINGS These are sometimes also called 'composite fats' and are generally packed under brand names. They are a mixture of fats such as fish oil, lard, soya bean oil and other vegetable fats which have been chemically refined and purified and then whipped or aerated. They are not considered to be wholefood ingredients.

CREAMED COCONUT This is pure coconut oil, which is sold in the form of a white block, and contains no additives or preservatives. It can be used for frying but is mostly used to enrich curries and as a substitute for cream in sweet dishes.

OILS Oils are becoming increasingly popular in the wholefood kitchen and many of them have a high proportion of polyunsaturated fats. The main difference between the many oils available is in the way they are extracted. The best oils are cold-pressed, which means that they have been obtained by simple pressing. They are a deep, rich colour, have the characteristic flavour of the original nuts and seeds and contain vitamins and minerals. The cheaper oils have gone through a process called solvent extraction in which they are dissolved out of the nuts and seeds with chemicals. Always buy a named oil. Those just labelled 'cooking' or 'vegetable' oils are a mixture of bad-tasting, solvent-extracted oils. The oils highest in polyunsaturated fats are safflower, sunflower, and soya bean oils. All these are excellent for cooking and for salads. Corn and groundnut oils are best used only for cooking as they do not have quite such a good flavour. Olive oil is probably the cook's favourite, and two more expensive but highly delicious salad oils are sesame and walnut.

Basic Wholefood Ingredients

Meat

Meat is an excellent source of protein, containing all the amino acids that we need. It contains B vitamins, including B_{12} which is only found elsewhere in eggs and, to a lesser extent, in soya beans and spinach. Red meats and offal are rich in iron and the lighter meats in potassium. The wholefood cook does not have to give up meat, but she may well use less as she becomes accustomed to all the other protein foods. She will also have to make sure that she uses good quality meat, since the lighter cooking methods will bring out the natural flavours.

The best meat that you can buy is that which has been naturally reared without the aid of hormones and anti-biotics. There are very few butchers in the country who sell only this type of meat, but many smaller butchers buy from local farms and it will probably pay you to ask a few questions before you decide on your regular source of supply. Don't forget game. Some types, such as rabbit and pigeon, are inexpensive and this is probably the most natural form of meat.

When cooking meat, use as little fat as possible. Grilling is an excellent method since all the fat can run away; and so is roasting if you use no basting fat and stand the meat on a rack in a roasting tin to cook. Pot roasts and casseroles are best made without browning the meat first, and you can make delicious dishes with a chicken or meat brick. Small amounts of cold meat can be mixed into salads with other protein foods, such as pulses or nuts, or serve plain sliced cooked meat with an imaginative side salad.

Fish

The wide variety that you see on the fishmonger's slab is all available to the wholefood cook. You can take your pick from oily fish, such as mackerel, herrings and fresh sardines, or white fish like cod, haddock and the cheaper coley. Shellfish are ideal for salads and first courses. You can choose cockles for everyday and prawns or crab for special occasions.

All fish is high in first class protein and valuable minerals, and most contain some B vitamins. White fish are rich in iodine, but contain no oils as these are confined to the liver. In oily fish, however, polyunsaturated fats are distributed throughout the fish and these contain high levels of vitamins A and D.

Breadcrumb and batter-coated fish, deep fried in oil and accompanied by fat-rich chips cannot be called a wholefood meal, but there are plenty of other ways of cooking. All fish can be grilled. White fish can be marinated first to make them moist and oily fish can be coated in wholemeal breadcrumbs or rolled oats and grilled completely without

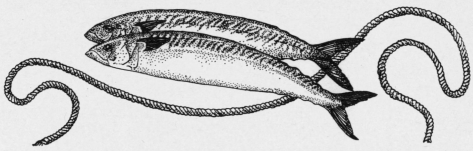

fat. If you bake fish, vinegar or lemon juice can be poured over oily fish to souse them, and white fish can be baked in wine or cider. You can also bake fish in packets of foil. All fish can be poached, and cold fish can be flaked into salads.

Eggs

Most people who like to eat natural foods would prefer free-range eggs. The yolks always seem darker and the shells stronger, and the very idea of buying a product of what amounts to a living, egg-producing machine can be off-putting.

However, only 1.8% of the eggs sold in this country are free-range. 2.5% are deep litter, which means the hens are kept in enclosed sheds but are free to run around. The rest are battery produced. Many of the free-range eggs are sold at the farm gate, wholefood shops can be good sources of supply and you can also buy them in some greengrocers. So have a good look round for possible sources. Eggs called 'Farm fresh' or 'Direct from the farm' need not necessarily be free-range. All eggs, in a sense, come from a farm, whether that farm has chicken runs or battery cages.

All eggs, free-range or not, provide first class protein that will supply us with all the essential amino acids. They contain vitamins A and D and all the B vitamins, especially B_{12} which is not frequently found in non-meat products. This makes them a valuable food for vegetarians. Eggs also contain a little vitamin E and the minerals calcium, potassium and magnesium. If you compare free-range and battery eggs you will find that the levels of fat, protein and some B vitamins are more or less the same but B_{12} is twice as high in free-range, and folic acid, another B vitamin, 50% higher. The vitamin E content differs widely both between and within the groups. Battery eggs are higher in iron, gained from the chickens pecking at their cage bars. They are also higher in calcium and sodium but there is more potassium in free-range.

Eggs must be one of the most versatile foods that any cook can lay her hands on. They can be boiled and served straight from the shell or with a savoury sauce or mayonnaise; poached and served on top of vegetables or smoked fish; scrambled alone or with additions such as mushrooms; baked and smothered with cheese; or made into dishes like filled omelettes, light soufflés and attractive roulades.

Dairy products

Dairy products include milk, cheese, cream, yogurt and buttermilk. Milk contains vitamin A, the B vitamins thiamin and riboflavin, a very little of vitamins C and D, a large amount of calcium and smaller quantities of other minerals such as potassium, phosphorus and iron. It also contains protein, fats and carbohydrates. Although we look on it more as a drink, it is really a complete food and is very versatile in the kitchen.

Some wholefood cooks prefer unsterilised or 'green-topped' milk. This is milk that has come straight from the cow without being treated in any way, so retaining all its original goodness and flavour. It is, however, relatively hard to come by, and so most of us have to be content with the ordinary pasteurised varieties, 'silver-topped' and 'gold-topped', which has a higher fat content.

In the pasteurisation process, milk is heated to 72°C (162°F), held there for 15 seconds and then rapidly cooled. About 10% of the B vitamins are lost and 25% of the vitamin C, but the other nutrients are unaffected.

Sterilised and UHT (ultra-high temperature), or 'long-life', milks have been treated to a greater extent and are thus not quite as nutritious as those which have only been pasteurised. Dried milk powder is made from skimmed, homogenised milk. It has a light effect in cooking and is useful to anyone on a low fat diet.

Goat's milk is becoming more popular and it can be drunk by many people who are allergic to cow's milk. It can be used in exactly the same ways as ordinary milk, and does not have as pronounced a flavour as you might expect.

Yogurt is milk which has undergone a fermentation process during which the milk sugars are broken down and the vitamins made more readily accessible to the body. It has virtually the same nutritional value as milk. Yogurt has become very popular in recent years and there are many different types on the market.

Most flavoured yogurts contain white sugar and some artificial colourings and flavourings. It is best to buy plain natural yogurt and flavour it yourself. The commercial varieties of yogurt may be made from milk, skimmed milk powder and liquid sucrose. Those to be found in wholefood shops are more likely to be made from milk alone.

Best of all, make your own yogurt (see page 207). It is very cheap and not at all difficult, and you will have the satisfaction of knowing what has gone into its making.

Cultured buttermilk is skimmed milk fermented with a culture in a similar way to yogurt. It is more liquid than yogurt and is sold in 300-ml ($\frac{1}{2}$-pint) cartons. You can drink it as it is or dilute it with water, and it is also excellent for baking.

Soured cream is also made with a culture. It has a high fat content but it is easier to digest than ordinary cream and it has a much lighter flavour. Double cream should only be used very occasionally in wholefood cooking.

There is a cheese for every occasion and to suit every purpose, and the wholefood cook can choose from the low fat cottage cheese, medium fat curd cheese and, on special occasions, cream cheese. In the hard cheese line there is medium fat Edam and the full fat traditional English cheeses such as Cheddar, Double Gloucester and Stilton. When you are choosing an English cheese, look out for the Farmhouse varieties. These have been made on the farm in a more traditional manner as opposed to in a factory, and their flavour is always superior.

Pulses

All the dried beans, peas and lentils are grouped together as pulses, and they come in all shapes, sizes and colours. Wholefood shops always have a good range and some of the more common ones can be found in supermarkets. Keep a good supply in your store-cupboard but always use them up within a year as after this they can become very tough.

All pulses contain the B group vitamins thiamin, riboflavin and niacin and the minerals iron and potassium. Soya beans also contain vitamins B_{12} and K and calcium. Most contain a high proportion of carbohydrates and only a trace of fat. Soya beans, on the other hand, have little carbohydrate and 18–22% polyunsaturated fat. All pulses contain protein. Soya beans contain first class protein and so can be eaten alone. The rest are lacking in certain amino acids and must be eaten with other foods containing protein, such as the whole grain products, bread, rice or wholemeal pasta.

The one drawback with many of the beans is the length of time that they take to soak and cook. You can simply soak them overnight, but if you don't remember, just bring them to the boil in enough water to cover, simmer them for 2 minutes and then leave them to soak in the water for 2–3 hours, until cold. Then add 30 ml (2 tbsp) oil to the water. This will prevent the beans foaming and give them a glossy texture. Bring the beans to the boil again and simmer them, covered, until tender. The time needed will depend on the type and age of bean (see chart on page 24). You can also put them for the same amount of time in a low oven. Do not use too much water for cooking the beans. Aim for most of it to be absorbed so that at the end you do not have to throw away the water-soluble vitamins that seep into it. No salt should be added during cooking as this will make the skins tough. All the flavourings should be added at the end.

Once the beans are cooked, you can use them in casseroles with vegetables in a similar way to meat, or you can make a thick sauce, stir in the beans and cook them for about 20 minutes. They can be rolled into pancakes and piled into pies and served mixed with tasty dressings in salads. Beans do not have to be the sole ingredient of a dish. They mix very well with meat or fish and often benefit from the addition of cheese. Beans can also be puréed and mixed with dressings to make tasty dips and spreads such as Middle Eastern hummus (see page 79).

Lentils and split peas need no soaking and they cook in 45 minutes–1 hour. Red lentils and split yellow and green peas are best made into thick soups, or purées which can be formed into patties and croquettes. The whole green and grey lentils can be made into similar dishes as the beans.

The chart below gives approximate times for cooking 225 g (8 oz) of the more common types of pulses until tender. First, soak the pulses overnight, or use the faster 'boiling' method (see page 23).

Type	Appearance	Cooking time
Haricot beans	Kidney-shaped, pale cream	$1-1\frac{1}{2}$ hours
Flageolet beans	Kidney-shaped, pale green	1 hour
Butter beans	Large, kidney-shaped, ivory	$1\frac{1}{2}$ hours
Chick peas	Round, pointed top, ivory	$1\frac{1}{2}-2$ hours
Black-eye beans	Small, kidney-shaped, cream with black spot	45 minutes–1 hour
Red kidney beans	Kidney-shaped, red	$1-1\frac{1}{2}$ hours
Brown kidney beans	Kidney-shaped, brown	1 hour
Black beans	Kidney-shaped, black, shiny	$1\frac{1}{2}$ hours
Aduki beans	Very small, round, red	30 minutes–1 hour
Mung (Moong) beans	Very small, round, green	40 minutes
Soya beans	Small, round, ivory, elongated when soaked	3–4 hours
Lentils	Small, red or larger greenish-brown	1 hour (no need to soak)
Split peas	Small green or yellow halved peas	45 minutes–1 hour (no need to soak)
Rose cocoa beans	Longish pink beans with darker flecks	1 hour
Cannellini beans	White, long beans	1 hour
Broad beans	Large, flat, brown	$1\frac{1}{2}-2$ hours
Foule beans	Thick skin, dull brown, about size of pea	$1-1\frac{1}{4}$ hours

PRESSURE COOKING BEANS If you have a pressure cooker, the process of cooking dried beans can be speeded up quite considerably.

Place the water in the pressure cooker. Allow at least 1.1 litres (2 pints) fresh cold water to every 450 g (1 lb) beans. The pressure cooker must be no more than half full. Bring the water to boiling point and add the beans. Bring to the boil again, uncovered, stirring frequently to prevent them sticking to the base, and remove any scum. Put on the lid, lower the heat so that the contents boil gently and bring to high (15 lb) pressure. Cook for the required time according to the chart below. Remove the cooker from the heat and reduce pressure slowly as the beans will rise and block the vent if the pressure is reduced quickly. Drain the beans and use as required.

Bean	Cooking time at high (15 lb) pressure	Bean	Cooking time at high (15 lb) pressure
Haricot beans	20 minutes	Brown kidney beans	20 minutes
Flageolet beans	20 minutes	Aduki beans	10 minutes
Butter beans	25 minutes	Cannellini beans	15 minutes
Chick peas	20 minutes	Rose cocoa beans	20 minutes
Black-eye beans	20 minutes	Lentils	15 minutes
Red kidney beans	20 minutes	Split peas	15 minutes

Soya products

Because the soya bean is such an excellent source of alternative protein, it has been made into various products, all of which can be a help to the wholefood cook. If you haven't the time to soak and cook whole soya beans you can buy soya 'splits' and soya 'grits', both of which are cooked, cracked soya beans. Splits look a little like chopped, skinned nuts. They cook in water without soaking in 45 minutes and can be used in exactly the same way as whole soya beans. The grits take the same time to cook, resulting in a light, fluffy purée which is best flavoured with herbs and spices and made into croquettes.

Tamari sauce is a soy sauce made solely from whole soya beans and sea salt. You can buy it from wholefood shops and it has a full, rich flavour far superior to any other type of soy sauce. In America it is called shoyu sauce.

Miso is a thick paste made from fermented soya beans which is added to meatless dishes after they are cooked in order to give flavour and extra protein. Several varieties can be found in wholefood shops including hacho, mugi, kome and genmai.

Tofu is soya bean curd which looks like the curd produced by adding rennet to milk. It is sold in a block about 2 cm ($\frac{3}{4}$ inch) thick and is often used in Chinese stir-fried dishes.

Fine, ivory-coloured soya flour can be added to cake and bread recipes for extra protein. You can also buy cans of soya milk which can be used in exactly the same way as ordinary milk and is useful for vegans (vegetarians who do not eat dairy products) and those allergic to cow's milk.

TVP (Textured Vegetable Protein), or spun soya beans, has not caught on as much as manufacturers once thought it would. It is a very processed product and not wholefood at all. It can also taste very unpleasant.

Nuts and seeds

If you are not a wholefood cook, you will most probably, up to now, have treated nuts more as an occasional nibble, garnish or stuffing ingredient than as the basis of a main meal. Nuts and seeds, such as sunflower, melon and sesame, are highly nutritious. The main vitamins they contain are A and those of the B group. Vitamins D, E and K are found in some. All nuts and seeds contain more minerals than meat, particularly potassium, phosphorus, iron and calcium. They are high in polyunsaturated fats and also in secondary protein. Nuts are a very concentrated source of goodness and are therefore best combined in some way with other ingredients such as breadcrumbs, vegetables and pulses to make dishes such as nut roasts, stir-fried dishes, croquettes and salads. In this way you will probably find that around 50 g (2 oz) nuts per person per meal is quite adequate, so making them a fairly cheap ingredient and not the expensive one that they would seem to be when you look at the price of 450 g (1 lb).

Nuts taste best when they are freshly shelled, but it's often hard to find the time to shell them all by hand, particularly if you need something like 225 g (8 oz) shelled nuts. It is best to buy them ready shelled from wholefood shops and store them in airtight jars. Do not buy more than a month's supply at a time since after that their flavour will deteriorate and they may start to go rancid.

Sprouted seeds and beans

When fresh salad ingredients are scarce it is always good to have your own supply, and this is quite possible even if you do not have a garden. Through seed catalogues and from wholefood shops you can buy seeds for sprouting in jam jars. The seeds, such as alfalfa and fenugreek, are sold singly or in special sandwich and salad mixtures. You can also sprout some of the dried beans, particularly aduki and mung beans, to produce bean sprouts which can be used raw or cooked.

You can buy special seed sprouters, but these are not absolutely necessary. All you need is a jam jar, a piece of muslin or nylon tights, an elastic band, a flat earthenware or pyrex dish and a large brown paper bag.

Put 15 ml (1 tbsp) of your chosen seeds or beans into the jar and cover the jar with the muslin or tights, anchored down with the elastic band. Pour warm water into the jar, rinse it round and pour it away. Fill the jar with warm water again and leave it for 24 hours. Pour away the water and rinse the seeds twice, discarding the water of the final rinse. Put the jar on its side on the dish, put the dish into the paper bag and leave in a warm place. Rinse and drain the seeds every morning and evening and in about 4 days the jar will be full of nutritious sprouts for salads and sandwiches. You can also add them to casseroles towards the end of the cooking time, mix them into breads or use them as garnish. Sprouts will keep in the jar in the refrigerator for up to 4 days. After that they tend to go bitter, and by then you should have the next batch ready.

Vegetables

Vegetable shops are the wholefood cook's treasure chest, providing a wealth of ingredients from the familiar to the exotic. Vegetables provide us with a whole selection of vitamins and minerals and as the amounts differ in each type it is best to eat a selection of different ones at every meal. Vitamin A is found in the red and orange coloured vegetables, particularly carrots, and also in green vegetables like broccoli, curly kale, spinach and cress. The B vitamins thiamin, nicotinic acid and riboflavin are in many green vegetables and vitamin C is high in most. The protein content of vegetables varies but it is highest in broad beans, peas and avocados. Carbohydrate is present in all vegetables in varying amounts. There are little or no fats in vegetables apart from avocados.

The best vegetables are those which have been organically grown without the aid of fertilizers or sprays, but unless you have a particularly well-stocked wholefood shop, know a reliable smallholder or farmer or, of course, grow your own, your supplies of these will never be certain. So shop around carefully for a greengrocer who gives good value. Never buy vegetables which look as though they have been picked for a long time as they will have lost some of their nutritional value. Store them in a cool, dry place and use them as soon as you can.

Fresh fruit

Fruit is sweet, low in calories and full of vitamins, so this is one sweet treat that we can all enjoy. The supply changes with the seasons, so giving us plenty of variety. The main vitamin in fruit is vitamin c and the yellow coloured ones like peaches are a good source of vitamin a. Vitamin k is found in the pith of citrus fruits. The minerals potassium and calcium are found in all fruits and there is also a small amount of iron.

You can eat fruit just as it is, straight from the bowl, or you can chop it up to make fruit salads or to be mixed into yogurt. You can make hot fruit compotes or more elaborate dishes such as pies and puddings and light, fluffy mousses.

If you don't care for sweet things or simply want to ring the changes, fruit can be used in savoury dishes. Mix it into salads or stir-fry it with vegetables. There is a school of thought which believes that man is best adapted for eating meat and fruit and certainly fruit acids do help to neutralise the fats that are found in meat. So you can make apple sauce or a fruit stuffing or cook the fruit in some way with grills and roasts.

Dried fruit

As all the water has been evaporated from them, dried fruits are much more concentrated in goodness than fresh. They contain b group vitamins and vitamin a and are particularly high in minerals, especially iron which is more easily digested than that in green vegetables.

Plastic-wrapped dried fruits always look very shiny and appetising, but they have been coated in an oil which may or may not be of vegetable origin and could even be liquid paraffin. This prevents the fruit from sticking together but it is thought by many people to be harmful. Whenever you can, buy oil-free fruits from wholefood shops and, if you are unable to find them, always wash the oil from the others by holding them in a colander under running warm water. Never keep dried fruit for more than a month or it may develop a sugary bloom. It will still be fine for cooking but will not be so appetising in salads and other uncooked dishes.

Dried fruits can be eaten instead of sweets and they provide a natural sweetness to all kinds of baking. They can be made into hot or cold dried fruit salads and they can also be added to savoury salads and stuffings.

Whole grains

Whole grains provide the 'filling' part of many wholefood meals, but they by no means contain only carbohydrate. They also consist of protein, B vitamins, and minerals such as phosphorus, potassium, iron and calcium. Wheat products also contain vitamin E. All whole grains are far richer in nutrients than refined grain products.

WHEAT Wheat is mostly used in the form of wholemeal flour. However, you can buy wheat grains. These you can cook in water in the oven very slowly and then make them into a savoury dish with onions and herbs or into a sweet dish. You can also buy 'kibbled' or cracked wheat which cooks more quickly. It can be soaked for about 6 hours, squeezed dry and served as a sweet or breakfast cereal with honey or yogurt. Wheat grains can be sprouted in jam jars (see page 26). They will be ready when the sprout is the same length as the grain and should then be used like rice or potatoes as an accompanying dish. They taste best either tossed in a salad dressing or mixed with herbs and onion.

BULGAR WHEAT (also called Bulgur or Burghul wheat) This is whole wheat grains that have been soaked and then toasted to a very high temperature until they crack. As a result they need little or no cooking. For a wheat salad to serve as a side dish, soak the bulgar in cold water for 30 minutes. Drain and squeeze it dry. Mix with a salad dressing and leave to stand for another 30 minutes before serving. For a cooked dish, skin and chop an onion and soften it in 60 ml (4 tbsp) oil in a saucepan. Raise the heat and stir in 225 g (8 oz) bulgar. Pour in 600 ml (1 pint) water or stock, season, cover and cook on a low heat for 20 minutes until the liquid is absorbed and the bulgar light and fluffy. You can also prepare it without the onion.

WHOLEMEAL SEMOLINA This is whole, coarsely ground, hard durum wheat (the type that is used for pasta). Use it in a similar way to white semolina to make delicious whole grain puddings. You can also use it in savoury salads in a similar way to bulgar, only it needs no initial soaking and is best mixed with a large proportion of vegetables such as tomatoes.

PASTA There is a wide range of wholewheat pastas on the market now. Spaghetti and lasagne are the most popular, but you can also buy macaroni, pasta rings and pasta twists. All wholewheat pastas take the same time to cook as white or spinach pastas (about 12–15 minutes in lightly salted simmering water). Buckwheat spaghetti is made from buckwheat flour. It is ideal for anyone allergic to wheat flour products and makes a pleasant change in any kitchen. It has a very mild buckwheat flavour and cooks in only 10 minutes.

RYE Whole rye grains are available from wholefood shops, but they are rarely used as a side dish. The most frequent use for rye is as a bread flour. It is best mixed half and half with wheat flour and makes a bread with a delicious nutty flavour.

BARLEY Whole barley grains are called pot barley and can be bought in wholefood shops. They can be cooked to make a savoury side dish or can have vegetables, meat or nuts added to make a complete grain-based meal. A simple way to cook barley is to skin and chop an onion and soften it in 60 ml (4 tbsp) oil in a flameproof casserole. Stir in 225 g (8 oz) pot barley and then 600 ml (1 pint) stock. Bring to the boil. Cover the casserole and cook in the oven at 180°C (350°F) mark 4 for 45 minutes. Herbs, spices and chopped vegetables can be added with the barley. Nuts are best added when cooking is completed.

Barley flour can be mixed half and half with wholemeal flour to make a light-coloured, slightly sweet bread.

OATS Whole grain oats are called oat groats and these can be cooked in the same way as pot barley. Oats are ground to make oatmeal of varying textures. Pin-head oatmeal is the coarsest form and it is used mainly for making porridge. Medium oatmeal also makes a good porridge and is the best type for making oatcakes, bannocks and parkin. Fine oatmeal is mostly mixed with wheat flour into bread, cake and biscuit mixtures. One quarter of oatmeal to three quarters of wholemeal flour is the right proportion. Both medium and fine oatmeals can be used for coating.

Rolled oats, sometimes called oat flakes, are produced by steam softening either oat

groats or pinhead oatmeal and then flattening them on a roller. They are most often used for muesli and for coarse biscuits of the flapjack variety.

MUESLI Ready-made muesli is sold in most supermarkets these days but many of the brands contain a high proportion of sugar. They can also be very highly priced. The best solution is to make your own. The base for muesli may consist only of rolled oats or a mixture of rolled oats, wheat, barley and rye. You can buy the base ready-mixed or the separate cereals for you to mix yourself. You can then add your own mixtures of nuts, fresh and dried fruits and raw sugar or honey (see page 236).

RICE Brown rice can be bought in long and short grain form and it may or may not

be organically grown. If it is, it will say so on the packet. Long grain brown rice is normally used only for savoury dishes; short grain can be used in the same way and it can also be made into brown rice puddings like white rice. When cooking brown rice, whether you are boiling or steaming it, remember that it takes 40–45 minutes to cook. It will be slightly chewy, never absolutely soft like white rice, and it is therefore always easier to get perfect results and evenly separated grains.

MILLET This is a small, yellow grain. Cook it like bulgar wheat (see page 28) and it will be light and fluffy. You can serve it plainly as a side dish or mix in vegetables, herbs or spices. With chopped nuts or diced meat it can make a substantial main dish. Savoury mixtures of millet can be made into croquettes and patties.

BUCKWHEAT Buckwheat groats are small heart-shaped seeds which are usually cooked in the same way as bulgar and millet to produce the dish called Kasha (see page 182). Buckwheat has a very strong, nutty flavour and is very much an acquired taste. It is also ground to make a fine, grey-coloured flour which is often used for yeasted pancakes.

Changing over to Wholefoods

Although it may seem impossible at first, it should not be too difficult to make the change to wholefoods. With a little forethought and organization, you will be able to plan your menus and shopping in just the same way as you always have, and wholefoods should not prove any more expensive. Once you have got used to the new flavours and textures you will want to experiment with different herbs and spices, introducing delicious new dishes for you and your family to enjoy.

Balancing the budget

One of the main arguments that you hear against changing the family over to wholefoods is that it will be very expensive. Some of the items you may have to buy do cost more, but you should also consider what you will *not* be buying.

Processed foods are amazingly expensive. For example, a small bag of potato crisps might seem a relatively cheap buy, but if you work it out you will find that they cost more than £1 for 450 g (1 lb), whereas you can buy 450 g (1 lb) of fresh potatoes in the winter for a few pence. All frozen, canned and dried vegetables are more expensive than their fresh counterparts; and it is certainly cheaper to make your own wholesome soups than to rely on packets and cans.

Wholemeal bread is, admittedly, more expensive than white, but it is much more satisfying so you will need less. You may also start to make your own which can be a considerable saving. Other wholemeal products, such as pasta, are also more satisfying than their white counterparts, and so too is brown rice. Bought pies made from white flour, whether sweet or savoury, always work out to be more expensive than home-baked wholemeal ones.

Muesli is the favourite wholefood breakfast cereal and if you buy it ready-mixed it will be more expensive than ordinary cereals. However, you can buy just the base and mix your own to make it more economical and also more suited to your particular taste.

Sweets and snacks should not feature in your shopping list at all so a great saving can be made here; and you will certainly be using less sugar and other sweeteners so the greater cost of raw sugar and honey over white sugar will be cancelled out. There is a wide range of wholemeal biscuits on the market now and they are, unfortunately, quite expensive, but if you regard them as an occasional treat rather than a regular item you will be spending less in the long run. Or you can always make your own wholemeal biscuits and cakes which will be very cheap.

Although meat and fish products such as fish fingers or beefburgers appear fairly inexpensive, if you compare the actual amount of meat and fish with fresh, they are not very good value for money. Canned stews and TV dinners work out far more expensive

31

than the same dishes made at home with fresh ingredients. Your wholefood menus will probably not include meat and fish every day of the week. You will also base meals on cheaper proteins such as eggs and cheese or combinations of the secondary protein foods like pulses and nuts.

Bought mousses, ice creams and other desserts, whether in pots or easy-mix packets will be left on the supermarket shelves and instead you will base your sweets more on fresh fruit and wholemeal baking. You can also make your own natural yogurt (see page 207) and flavour it with fresh fruit or use it as a substitute for the more expensive and not so healthy cream.

Herbs and spices are as invaluable to the wholefood cook as to any other, and they are relatively cheap as long as you buy them loose or in plain containers. You can also grow herbs yourself at very little cost, so you can always have them fresh. With these there will be no need for packeted and canned sauces; and if you make your own stock, there will be no need for foil-wrapped cubes.

You should, by the end of your shopping day, find that you are saving a little money by sticking to wholefoods, or at any rate breaking even. If not, should you really complain? The food you have bought is contributing to your family's health and general well-being and as such is a worthwhile investment.

Shopping wisely

You don't have to do all your shopping at expensive wholefood shops but you will have to go to them sometimes. Prices can vary considerably between these shops so if you have several in your district it will pay you to have a good look round first before you become a regular at any one of them. Probably the best are the wholefood cooperatives who buy big sacks of everything, from dried fruits to pulses, from wholesalers and then weigh them out themselves. From these shops you will probably be able to buy some of the commodities that you regularly use in bulk, and so save a few pennies. Rice, pasta and pulses will keep for up to a year; so will tahini (sesame paste); and honey will keep indefinitely, although liquid honey, if kept in a cool place, may crystallise. Oils bought in 5-litre (9-pint) cans will keep well provided you use them steadily, but it is best if you buy only enough dried fruits and nuts to last you a month. Wholemeal flour is available in 25-kg (55-lb) sacks, and it is definitely cheaper, but do remember that after about 6 weeks it starts to deteriorate. If you only use about 1.4 kg (3 lb) a week, it is best to buy it in small bags.

Since fresh fruit and vegetables are going to make up a sizeable proportion of your weekly shopping, look around at your local greengrocers for the one who gives you the best combination of economy, quality and freshness. Markets are also a good source of supply, provided you watch carefully that you get the items you asked for and not the rather dreary specimens at the back of the stall! In the summer it is fun to take advantage of the 'pick-your-own' advertisements that you see, but only buy large

Dried beans (*page 23*)

quantities of the vegetables and fruits that will store well such as apples and root vegetables. It is good neither for your health or your purse if any go stale before you manage to eat them.

Fresh fish is generally no problem since most fishmongers have good quality wares, but you may have to look around for meat. Some supermarket meat is very good, but you can't ask for the amount that you want or for a specific cut if you can't see it on the shelves. Neither can you see the side of the meat which is against the wrapping. In general, the small family butchers are the best for meat. They often buy whole fresh animals and cut them up themselves. If you have a freezer and know a local farmer or smallholder who will let you have half a sheep or pig, then it will be very economical to buy in this way and you have the advantage of knowing where your meat came from. Bulk buys from freezer centres, however, may not be a good idea. If the meat is of bad quality you have made an expensive mistake.

Supermarkets are getting better all the time and most now stock wholemeal bread and flour. But you may find that shopping in smaller shops is more fun and that in some cases you are getting better value for money by shopping around a little.

Planning menus and serving wholefood

Whichever form of cooking you prefer, it is always best to vary your menus as much as possible, then you will not be bored with cooking, and your family will continue to eat with enthusiasm. The secret of success is to choose something different every day from the many different basic ingredients available to the wholefood cook (see page 20). It might even help, if you are a beginner, to sit down and plan a week's menus in advance. Alternate meat, fish and non-meat days; and on some days have a first course and a main dish, while on others start with the main dish and end with a sweet. If your main dish is cooked, then have a salad to begin with, or have a hot first course or a soup before a salad. Always have a selection of different vegetables, have a side salad at at least one meal a day, and occasionally serve pasta, rice and grain dishes as a change from potatoes. On some days you can make these accompanying foods into the basis of a hearty all-in-one main dish.

In order to tempt your family into eating what to them may be new foods, make your dishes look attractive. Arrange them temptingly on serving dishes and garnish them with vegetables or chopped herbs.

Choose a sweet that will suit the rest of the meal. Fresh fruit or a light fruit compote will be quite enough if the meal has been on the heavy side; or if you are to have a light egg dish, for example, or a salad, a more substantial pudding may be called for.

Don't serve portions that are too large at first. Wholefood meals can be very filling, and struggling with too much may easily put off both children and adults.

If you follow these simple guidelines, your family can look forward to many nutritious, varied and enjoyable meals.

From top: Wholemeal croissants (*page 40*), Haddock kedgeree, Honey fruit muesli (*page 46*)

Why no convenience foods?

Many convenience foods contain additives. These can be described as substances that are put into food, which have no nutritional value, but which change the nature of the food in some way. There are about three thousand permitted additives used by British manufacturers. Some are completely natural substances such as herbs and spices or vitamin C, but most are chemical. They can be divided into eight groups: flavourings, flavour enhancers such as monosodium glutamate, thickeners and stabilisers, emulsifiers, food acids, colourings, preservatives and sweeteners. There are strict controls over which ones are allowed on the permitted list, but the list is continually being changed as harmful effects, hitherto unnoticed, are coming to light after perhaps years of use. Eating one food that contains an additive will do no harm to anyone, but if convenience foods make up a large proportion of your diet, there could be a significant build-up. Children are most at risk because they have a lower body weight and so they receive larger quantities in proportion to adults.

Canned, frozen and dried foods are all less nutritious than fresh. Before canning, vegetables are peeled, which cuts down on fibre and exposes the surface to the air, so beginning the loss of vitamins. They might also be cleaned by hot steam which destroys vitamins B and C, or with a chemical solution. Then they are chopped, sliced or diced and probably soaked in water, causing more vitamins to escape. They are blanched and a preservative such as sulphur dioxide may or may not be added. This helps to preserve vitamin C but destroys thiamin. They are put in water in the cans and cooked (more vitamins are lost here) and then salt, sugar and colouring may be added. The longer the vegetables are stored in the tin, the more vitamins will seep into the liquid, and this is the part that we usually throw away. Packets of dried vegetables have probably lost

more vitamins and minerals than vegetables preserved in other ways. Instant mashed potato, for example, contains no vitamin c at all.

Freezing is the newest and fastest method of preserving. The vegetables are subject to the same peeling and chopping process, and they are also blanched, but no chemicals are added. Sugar or sugar syrup is generally added to frozen fruits and a chemically treated pectin called methyl pectin may be used to treat raspberries and strawberries. All food must be frozen quickly. If not, large ice crystals will form and vitamins will be lost on thawing. The longer frozen vegetables are stored, the greater the vitamin c loss.

Fish freezes very well and, by law, contains no additives. Some fish products, however, are coated in coloured breadcrumbs.

Frozen meat, as opposed to meat products, is also additive-free, but after six months there is a 20–40% thiamin loss. Oven-ready frozen poultry is very often injected with polyphosphates which prohibit the growth of bacteria and which also prevent loss of water during cooking. Meat products and TV dinners may be only 66% lean meat. Most of them contain monosodium glutamate and anti-oxidants.

Fresh foods are definitely more nutritious than processed, and using them to make a large variety of dishes will not only contribute greatly to your family's health but will also give far more enjoyment.

Adding flavour

Wholefoods are not dull unless you make them so, and most of the flavourings that are available to the gourmet cook can also be used in the wholefood kitchen.

Herbs provide many different flavours from the soft and mild to the very pungent, and they are also a good source of minerals and trace elements. Most enthusiastic cooks have their own herb garden and if you haven't perhaps now is the time to start. It is surprising how many herbs can be fitted into a small plot, and if no garden is available then you can grow them perfectly well in window boxes and flower pots. If you have to use dried herbs, halve the amount given in a recipe for fresh and use within six months.

A bouquet garni consists of a few sprigs of culinary herbs tied together with cotton or string in a small bouquet. It takes very little time to make from fresh herbs. You can also buy small muslin bags and paper sachets of herbs which you can use instead.

Many recipes can be improved by spices. Small amounts will do us no harm but heavily spiced food such as really strong, spicy curries, eaten too often may overload the system. Some spices, like ginger and cayenne pepper, can only be bought ground, and it is impractical to grind your own cinnamon. Nutmegs are best bought whole and grated as you need them, and allspice, cloves and juniper berries can easily be crushed with a pestle and mortar. Pepper is best freshly ground from a mill.

Try not to use too much salt in your cooking and when you do, use a sea salt or natural rock salt. These contain many natural minerals and no additives to make them flow freely. If you find the salt too coarse, use a salt mill.

The many spiced mustards that you can buy now can be mixed into salad dressings and cooked dishes. Pickles such as gherkins and capers give added piquancy to dishes that might otherwise be rather bland, such as those made with beans. Olives and anchovies give authentic Italian flavours, and tomato purée, Worcestershire sauce and tamari sauce all help to make wholefood cooking really exciting.

Breakfast
with a Smile

Everyone feels differently in the mornings. There are some who wake up feeling ravenous and ready to go and there are the slower starters who maintain that they cannot face anything other than coffee at breakfast time. When we get up in the morning, unless we have had a really large meal quite late the night before, most of us have not eaten for around twelve hours and our energy levels are low. If we launch straight into a busy working day without eating anything we will not be able to keep going for as long and with as much enthusiasm as we would if we had spared the time to 'break our fast'. Surveys show that we might even be more accident-prone.

You don't have to start with cereal, work your way through a fry-up and end with toast and marmalade. Even small breakfasts, so long as you combine your ingredients well, can be extremely nourishing, and if you don't even feel like eating, you can combine such foods as yogurt, fruit juice, eggs, milk and honey in a blender so all you have to do is sit down and have a drink.

It is perfectly possible to have a wholefood 'continental' breakfast. Eat wholemeal toast or make your own wholemeal croissants (see page 40). Spread them lightly with butter, vegetable margarine or peanut butter (see page 66), and, instead of jam, use honey or one of the new sugar-free fruit spreads that you can buy in wholefood shops. For a savoury change, put a pot of yeast extract, such as Marmite or Barmene, on the table.

The most popular breakfast is some kind of cereal, partly because it is so easy to tip it from the packet and top it with sugar and milk. Most cereals are over-processed and they also lead you to eat too much sugar, so the best way to overcome this is to mix your own muesli (see page 236). Everyone's tastes differ so it is a good idea to put a bowl of muesli base on the table together with bowls of dried fruits, nuts, fresh fruit, raw sugar

or honey and a jug of milk or home-made yogurt (see page 207) so everyone can have fun mixing their own. However, if you think this might be too time-consuming, you can mix up enough for the whole family the night before.

Porridge is a hot and warming cereal to have first thing in the morning and it is most nutritious made from coarse or medium oatmeal which can be put to soak overnight for quick cooking in the morning. Top it with demerara sugar or honey.

Fruit makes a refreshing start in the morning. You can simply sit and munch on an apple, or you can chop fruit the night before and mix it with a little honey to make a fruit salad. For extra goodness you can top it with wheatgerm or chopped nuts or spoon over some natural yogurt.

Yogurt alone is nourishing and light. You can dilute it with fruit juice to make a drink, or you can mix in fresh or dried fruits, fruit purées, chopped nuts, honey or wheatgerm to make it more satisfying.

If you have the time and appetite for a cooked breakfast, then try to make your cooking methods as light and fat-free as possible. Eggs are perfect at breakfast time as we digest them very slowly and they keep us going for a long while. Simply soft-boiled with 'soldiers' of wholemeal toast, eggs can be absolutely superb, or you can poach, scramble or bake them. Bacon can be grilled and served on wholemeal toast instead of with fried bread and, for a treat, try poached or grilled kippers.

If we start the day right, whatever we do throughout the day will work out well; and this does not only apply to what we eat. Whenever possible, make breakfast a time when all the family meets together and enjoys themselves; and even get up that little bit earlier in order to do so. Then you will feel healthy and happy for the rest of the day.

Breakfast in a glass

5 ml (1 level tsp) coffee substitute
300 ml ($\frac{1}{2}$ pint) milk
1 egg
5 ml (1 tsp) clear honey

Put the coffee substitute and milk in a saucepan. Bring to the boil and simmer for 1 minute. Strain through a fine sieve, then pour into a blender with the egg and honey and blend well. Alternatively, thoroughly whisk in the egg and honey until smooth. Serve immediately.

Serves 1

Orange and honey vitaliser

juice of 2 oranges
1 egg yolk
5 ml (1 tsp) clear honey

Pour the orange juice into a jug and beat in the egg yolk and honey. Alternatively, place all the ingredients in a blender and blend for 30 seconds. Serve immediately.

Serves 1

Wholemeal croissants

Illustrated in colour on page 34

25 g (1 oz) fresh or 15 g ($\frac{1}{2}$ oz) dried yeast
400 ml ($\frac{3}{4}$ pint) warm milk and water mixed
550 g (1 lb 4 oz) plain wholemeal flour
2.5 ml ($\frac{1}{2}$ level tsp) freshly ground sea salt
315 g (11$\frac{1}{2}$ oz) vegetable margarine
1 egg, beaten

Blend the yeast with 150 ml ($\frac{1}{4}$ pint) milk and water and leave for about·15 minutes until frothy. Mix the flour and salt together and stir in the yeast mixture. Melt 40 g (1$\frac{1}{2}$ oz) margarine and add to the flour with enough of the remaining milk and water to make a fairly soft dough. Knead lightly, then cover and leave in a warm place to rise for about 30 minutes until doubled in size.

Turn the dough on to a floured surface and knead lightly. Roll into an oblong measuring 18 × 53.5 cm (7 × 21 inches), keeping the edges straight. Soften the remaining margarine with a knife and divide into three portions. Dot one portion of margarine over the top two thirds of the dough in small pieces so that it looks like buttons on a card. Fold the bottom third of the dough up and the top third down, sealing the edges well with a rolling pin, and turn it so that the folded edges are at the side.

Roll out again into an oblong, dot over the second portion of margarine, fold and turn as before. Repeat with the final portion of margarine. Between the rollings, cover the dough and leave in the refrigerator for about 20 minutes, so that the fat does not become too soft with over-handling.

Finally, roll out the dough quite thinly and cut into triangles, with sides longer than bases, measuring about 23 × 23 × 15 cm (9 × 9 × 6 inches). Roll up each triangle, starting from the base and curl the ends round to form a crescent. Put on to greased baking sheets, cover and leave to rise for 15–20 minutes until doubled in size. Brush with egg and bake in the oven at 230°C (450°F) mark 8 for 10–15 minutes until risen.

Makes about 16

Hot bacon and cottage cheese sandwiches

225 g (8 oz) lean unsmoked bacon, rinded
8 slices of granary bread
a little vegetable margarine
225 g (8 oz) cottage cheese with chives
25 g (1 oz) walnuts, roughly chopped

Grill the bacon until crisp, then roughly snip into pieces. Toast the bread slices and spread one side of each with a little margarine. Sprinkle the bacon over four slices of the toast. Mix the cottage cheese and walnuts together and spoon over the bacon. Sandwich together with the remaining four slices of toast. Cut in half and serve immediately.

Serves 4

Stuffed mushrooms

16 medium mushrooms, wiped
2 small onions, skinned and finely chopped
25 g (1 oz) butter or vegetable margarine
175 g (6 oz) ham, trimmed of fat and finely chopped
150 g (5 oz) fresh wholemeal breadcrumbs
50 g (2 oz) Cheddar cheese, grated
10 ml (2 level tsp) chopped fresh parsley
1 egg, beaten
freshly ground sea salt and pepper
4 slices of wholemeal bread, toasted and lightly buttered

Remove and chop the stalks from the mushrooms. Lightly fry the mushroom stalks and onion in the fat for 3–5 minutes, until soft but not brown. Add the ham, breadcrumbs, cheese and parsley and enough egg to bind them all together. Stir until well mixed and hot, season to taste and pile into the mushroom caps. Put the mushrooms, filling side up, on a greased baking sheet and bake in the oven at 190°C (375°F) mark 5 for about 20 minutes or until the mushrooms are tender. Serve on buttered toast.

Serves 4

Peach nectar

225 g (8 oz) fresh peaches, skinned, stoned and quartered
juice of 1 orange
30 ml (2 tbsp) lemon juice
15 ml (1 tbsp) clear honey
about 300 ml ($\frac{1}{2}$ pint) water

Purée the peaches in a blender with the orange juice, lemon juice and honey. Pour into a large jug and add enough water to dilute to taste. Chill and serve.

Serves 4

Hot breakfast fruits

100 g (4 oz) prunes
150 g (5 oz) dried apricots
50 g (2 oz) seedless raisins
2 bananas, peeled and cut into chunks
45 ml (3 tbsp) clear honey
grated rind and juice of 1 lemon
60 ml (4 tbsp) orange juice
15 g ($\frac{1}{2}$ oz) butter

Soak the prunes and apricots overnight in enough water to cover. The next day, drain
the fruit and stone the prunes. Place them in an ovenproof dish with the raisins and
bananas. Spoon the honey, lemon rind and juice over the fruit and stir in the orange
juice. Dot the butter over the top and bake in the oven at 180°C (350°F) mark 4 for
about 30 minutes or until the fruit is soft. Serve plain or with natural yogurt.

Serves 4

Toasted oat muesli

100 g (4 oz) rolled oats, toasted
150 ml ($\frac{1}{4}$ pint) milk
25 g (1 oz) crunchy wheatgerm
50 g (2 oz) walnuts, roughly chopped
25 g (1 oz) sultanas
50 g (2 oz) stoned dates, roughly chopped
1 eating apple, cored and roughly diced
60 ml (4 tbsp) clear honey
300 ml ($\frac{1}{2}$ pint) natural yogurt
30 ml (2 tbsp) lemon juice

Place the oats and milk in a bowl and leave to soak overnight. The next day, mix in the
wheatgerm, walnuts, sultanas, dates and apple. Stir the honey, yogurt and lemon juice
together and stir into the muesli, adding more milk if desired. Serve in cereal bowls.

Serves 4

Banana and bacon rolls

8 rashers of lean unsmoked bacon, rinded
2 bananas, peeled
4 slices of wholemeal bread, toasted and lightly buttered

Stretch the bacon rashers with a knife and cut each in half. Cut the bananas into sixteen
large chunks. Roll the rashers round the banana chunks and grill until the bacon is
cooked. Serve with fingers of lightly buttered wholemeal toast.

Serves 4

Grilled grapefruit and orange cups

2 grapefruit, halved
60 ml (4 tbsp) natural yogurt or soured cream
1.25 ml ($\frac{1}{4}$ level tsp) ground cinnamon
60 ml (4 level tbsp) demerara sugar
1 orange, peeled and segmented

Scoop the flesh out of the grapefruit halves, reserving the empty shells and any juice for a fruit drink (*eg*. Honey fruit punch on page 241). Roughly chop the grapefruit flesh and stir in the natural yogurt or soured cream, the cinnamon and half the sugar. Pile into the grapefruit shells and arrange the orange segments on top. Sprinkle with the remaining sugar. Place under a hot grill until the sugar is golden. Serve immediately.

Serves 4

Mackerel and apple crispbreads

225 g (8 oz) smoked mackerel
1 large eating apple, cored
150 ml ($\frac{1}{4}$ pint) mayonnaise (see page 171)
freshly ground sea salt and pepper
30 ml (2 tbsp) lemon juice
8 rye crispbreads

Remove the skin and any bones from the fish and break it up slightly. Finely dice half the apple and add to the fish. Mix the mayonnaise with the seasoning and 15 ml (1 tbsp) lemon juice and stir into the fish. Mix well, then spoon equally on to the crispbreads. Cut the remaining apple half into thin slices, dip them in the remaining lemon juice to prevent discoloration, and use to garnish the mackerel.

Serves 4

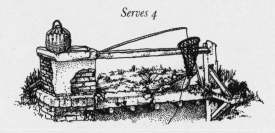

Oatmeal porridge

1.1 litres (2 pints) water
150 g (5 oz) medium oatmeal
5 ml (1 level tsp) freshly ground sea salt

Bring the water to the boil in a large saucepan. Gradually add the oatmeal, stirring all the time. Cover the pan and simmer for 10 minutes. Add the salt and simmer for a further 10–20 minutes until cooked. Serve with milk and demerara sugar.

Serves 4

Cheese scramble

4 rashers of lean unsmoked bacon, rinded .
100 g (4 oz) mushrooms, wiped and chopped
4 eggs, beaten
freshly ground sea salt and pepper
60 ml (4 tbsp) milk
25 g (1 oz) butter or vegetable margarine
100 g (4 oz) Cheddar cheese, grated
4 slices of granary bread, toasted

Place the bacon and mushrooms in the grill pan and grill under a medium heat for about 5 minutes, turning occasionally, until tender.

Beat the eggs, seasoning and milk together. Melt the fat in a saucepan and pour in the eggs. Cook gently, stirring, over a low heat until set. Stir in the cheese just before the egg sets. Place a bacon rasher on each slice of toast and spoon over the cheesy scrambled egg. Top with the grilled mushrooms.

Serves 4

Grilled kidneys and mushrooms

30 ml (2 tbsp) sunflower oil
30 ml (2 tbsp) lemon juice
freshly ground sea salt and pepper
15 ml (1 tbsp) Worcestershire sauce
450 g (1 lb) lambs' kidneys, skinned and cored
100 g (4 oz) button mushrooms, wiped and sliced
2 tomatoes, skinned and quartered

Mix the oil, lemon juice, seasonings and Worcestershire sauce together. Cut the kidneys into quarters and mix with the mushrooms and tomatoes. Place in a grill pan and pour over the dressing. Put under a pre-heated grill and cook for 5–6 minutes, stirring from time to time to prevent drying out. Serve hot with the juices, accompanied by hot toast.

Serves 4

Baked eggs

50 g (2 oz) butter
4 eggs
freshly ground sea salt and pepper

Place four individual ovenproof dishes or cocottes on a baking sheet, and put a quarter of the butter in each. Put them in the oven for 1–2 minutes, until the butter has melted. Break an egg into each dish and sprinkle with a little salt and pepper. Bake in the oven at 180°C (350°F) mark 4 for 5–8 minutes until the eggs are just set. Serve at once.

Serves 4

Shirred eggs with chicken livers

225 g (8 oz) chicken livers
60 ml (4 tbsp) tomato juice
4 eggs
freshly ground sea salt and pepper
chopped fresh parsley to garnish

Line a grill pan with foil and gently grill the chicken livers for about 5 minutes, tossing occasionally, to seal. Roughly chop the livers and use to line four ramekin dishes. Pour 15 ml (1 tbsp) tomato juice into each, then break an egg in on top. Sprinkle with salt and pepper and bake in the oven at 180°C (350°F) mark 4 for 10 minutes, until the egg is set. Sprinkle with chopped parsley and serve.

Serves 4

Smoked haddock omelette

2 eggs
freshly ground sea salt and pepper
15 g ($\frac{1}{2}$ oz) butter

For the filling
50–75 g (2–3 oz) cooked smoked haddock
25 g (1 oz) Cheddar cheese, grated

Lightly whisk the eggs, 15 ml (1 tbsp) water and the seasoning together. Melt the butter in a frying pan over a moderate heat, tilting the pan so that the inside surface is evenly greased. Pour in the egg mixture and gently stir with a fork, allowing the uncooked egg to flow to the sides and cook. Once the egg has set, stop stirring and cook the omelette for another minute, until the under-side is golden brown.

For the filling, flake the cooked haddock and stir in the cheese. Drop the filling on to the centre of the omelette and, using a palette knife, fold the omelette by flicking one third over to the centre, then fold over the opposite side. Turn the omelette on to a hot plate, folded side underneath, to serve.

Serves 1

Grapefruit wake-me-up

juice of 1 grapefruit
15 ml (1 level tbsp) demerara sugar
1 egg

Place all the ingredients in a blender and blend for 30 seconds. Alternatively, whisk the ingredients together in a bowl. Serve immediately.

Serves 1

Haddock kedgeree

Illustrated in colour on page 34

175 g (6 oz) brown rice
350 g (12 oz) smoked haddock
2 hard-boiled eggs
75 g (3 oz) butter or vegetable margarine
freshly ground sea salt and pepper
chopped fresh parsley to garnish

Cook the rice the night before. Bring a large saucepan of lightly salted water to the boil. Stir in the rice, cover and simmer for 40–45 minutes or until the rice is just tender. Drain, rinse in cold water to stop the cooking process and drain again. Leave to cool completely, then store overnight in a covered polythene container in the refrigerator.

The next day, put the haddock in a large bowl or jug and cover with boiling water. Leave for 10–15 minutes or until the haddock is tender, then drain, skin and flake the fish. Chop one egg and slice the other into rings. Melt the fat in a pan, add the rice, fish, chopped egg, salt and pepper and stir over a moderate heat for about 5 minutes or until hot. Pile on to a warmed serving dish and garnish with parsley and sliced egg.

Serves 4

Honey fruit muesli

Illustrated in colour on page 34

25 g (1 oz) rolled oats
150 ml ($\frac{1}{4}$ pint) milk
3 oranges
3 eating apples, cored
30 ml (2 level tbsp) sultanas
1 banana, peeled and sliced
30 ml (2 level tbsp) ground almonds
15 ml (1 tbsp) clear honey
60 ml (4 tbsp) natural yogurt
a few black and green grapes, halved and pipped

Place the oats and milk in a bowl and leave to soak overnight. The next day, add the juice from one of the oranges and grate the apples into the oats. Peel and segment the other two oranges and roughly chop. Stir the sultanas, banana, almonds, honey, yogurt, oranges and grapes into the oat and apple mixture. Serve chilled.

Serves 4

Swiss apple muesli

40 g (1½ oz) rolled oats or medium oatmeal
150 ml (¼ pint) orange juice
2 eating apples
60 ml (4 tbsp) milk
15 ml (1 tbsp) thick honey
a little demerara sugar
50 g (2 oz) sultanas or seedless raisins
a few chopped nuts, *eg*. almonds, walnuts or hazelnuts

Place the oats and orange juice in a bowl and leave to soak overnight. The next day, grate the apples and mix into the oats with the rest of the ingredients except the nuts. Serve in bowls, sprinkled with chopped nuts.

Serves 4

Latticed ham and egg toasts

4 slices of lean ham
4 slices of granary bread, toasted and lightly buttered
25 g (1 oz) vegetable margarine
4 eggs, beaten
60 ml (4 tbsp) milk
freshly ground sea salt and pepper

Cut the ham slices in half and put half a slice on each piece of toast. Cut the remaining half slices into strips.

Melt the margarine in a saucepan. Beat the eggs, milk, salt and pepper together and pour into the saucepan. Cook gently, stirring, until set, then spoon the scrambled egg on to the toast slices. Garnish with a lattice of ham strips and serve immediately.

Serves 4

Cheese and tomato toasted sandwiches

8 slices of wholemeal bread
butter or vegetable margarine
4 thin slices of Cheddar cheese
4 tomatoes, sliced
15 ml (1 level tbsp) chopped fresh chives

Spread the slices of bread with a little butter or vegetable margarine. Put a slice of cheese, tomato slices and a sprinkling of chives on each of four slices of bread and sandwich together with the other slices. Put under a pre-heated grill and toast both sides. Serve immediately.

Serves 4

Wholemeal pancakes with orange and honey

100 g (4 oz) plain wholemeal flour
1.25 ml ($\frac{1}{4}$ level tsp) freshly ground sea salt
1 egg, beaten
150 ml ($\frac{1}{4}$ pint) milk
150 ml ($\frac{1}{4}$ pint) water
sunflower oil
45 ml (3 tbsp) clear honey
15 ml (1 tbsp) lemon juice
2 oranges, peeled and segmented
2 bananas, peeled and sliced

Sift the flour and salt together into a bowl. Make a well in the centre and gradually pour in the egg and milk, beating after each addition. Beat until the batter is smooth, then add the water. Add more water if necessary to give a 'dropping' consistency.

Heat 2.5 ml ($\frac{1}{2}$ tsp) sunflower oil in a small frying pan. When very hot, pour off the excess oil and pour in enough batter to thinly coat the base of the pan. Cook gently until the under-side of the pancake is golden brown. Turn it over with a palette knife or by tossing and cook the second side until golden brown. Turn out on to greaseproof paper and repeat until eight pancakes are made, oiling the pan again when necessary.

Heat the honey and lemon juice in a saucepan and stir in the orange segments and banana slices. Coat well in the honey, then divide equally on to the centre of each hot pancake. Carefully flip two sides of each pancake over the filling and serve immediately.

Makes 8

Crispy bacon pancakes

100 g (4 oz) plain wholemeal flour
freshly ground sea salt and pepper
2 eggs, beaten
150 ml ($\frac{1}{4}$ pint) milk
30 ml (2 tbsp) sunflower oil
175 g (6 oz) lean unsmoked bacon, rinded and finely chopped
1 small onion, skinned and finely chopped
50 g (2 oz) mushrooms, wiped and finely chopped

Sift the flour and seasoning together into a bowl. Make a well in the centre and gradually pour in the eggs and half the milk, beating after each addition. Beat until the batter is smooth, then add the remaining milk. If necessary, add a little more milk so that the batter is of a 'dropping' consistency.

Heat half the oil in a large frying pan and sauté the bacon, onion and mushrooms for 5 minutes until soft. Remove from the pan with a slotted spoon and stir the bacon mixture into the batter. Heat the remaining oil in the pan and drop 30 ml (2 tbsp) mixture into the pan for each pancake. Cook on each side for about 3 minutes or until golden brown. Turn on to greaseproof paper, keep warm and repeat. Serve immediately.

Makes about 10

Lunch and
Supper Dishes

One big meal a day is generally enough for anybody and the remaining meal will either be lunch or supper, depending on whether you eat your main meal in the middle of the day or in the evening. Whichever it is, it will need to be light, but nevertheless nourishing and, if you are at home, the food you will serve at either meal will be very similar.

However, if most of your family are out for lunch, then you will have to decide whether to leave it to the school, the canteen or, in some cases, the pub to provide them with their mid-day sustenance, or whether to pack them up something to take.

If you can, check up first on the type of school meals offered. Some school and canteen lunches can be very substantial but it is rare that even a thought is given as to whether they are wholefood or not. Giving children money to buy their own isn't a very good idea either as, when with friends, they can easily be tempted into buying bags of crisps and sticky white buns.

Pub lunches can be good. A wholemeal sandwich or a salad and half a pint of real ale or a fruit or tomato juice makes a nutritious snack, but two stiff gins and a greasy pie are not quite so wholesome! If your husband can't change his pub, then pack up a few small sandwiches for him to eat in the middle of the day.

Business lunches can be a problem, both for the working wife who has to come home afterwards and make a meal for her family when she herself doesn't feel like eating it, and for the husband who eats so much at lunch time that he cannot face the large meal his wife prepares in the evening. The best solution, if you still want your evening meal, is first of all to drink very little and, secondly, to choose the lightest things on the menu. Grapefruit and melon make ideal starters for these occasions and, if there is no salad offered for the main course, ask if you could possibly have one of the light fish dishes, listed as a first course, as a main meal. Most restaurants will be happy to oblige.

To get back to the lunch box, if sandwiches are to be the main item, always make them wholemeal. Try to make them interesting and vary the filling every day; and put the same fillings between crispbreads for any slimmers. If your family are offered facilities for eating packed lunches, you can pack them up a salad in a plastic box so they can eat it with a fork. If not, make sure you put in a couple of tomatoes and an apple.

You can also make all-in-one salads by mixing various ingredients such as diced or grated cheese, chopped nuts, cold meat or flaked fish into brown rice with various chopped vegetables or, for a lighter meal, again suitable for slimmers, you can make mixtures based on cottage cheese. For cold days, make some home-made soup for them to take in a thermos flask.

If you are staying at home for lunch, or if your light meal is in the evening, then these sandwiches, salads and substantial soups are just as suitable, but you will also have the opportunity to make perhaps more elaborate salads or something hot. Toast is a delicious lunch and supper time standby. You can spread various sandwich mixtures over toast, or top it with cheese or grilled vegetables such as mushrooms or tomatoes. If you prefer potatoes to bread, bake them in their jackets, scoop out the fillings and mix them with something savoury (see page 57).

Many quick and easy dishes can be made with eggs, such as an omelette for the one person at home alone or a large quiche for when friends are dropping round.

None of the dishes for this light meal of the day should be too complicated or you will end up spending just as much time on this as on the main meal, but they should all be attractive and very appetising so everyone in the family will be well nourished throughout the day.

Avocado and grapefruit salad (*page 73*), Herb oatcakes (*page 234*)

Smoked haddock flan

175 g (6 oz) wholemeal pastry (see page 237)
225 g (8 oz) smoked haddock fillets
juice of $\frac{1}{2}$ a lemon
25 g (1 oz) butter
50 g (2 oz) mushrooms, wiped and sliced
2 eggs
45 ml (3 tbsp) milk
100 g (4 oz) cottage cheese
freshly ground sea salt and pepper

Roll out the pastry and use to line a 20.5-cm (8-inch) flan ring. Prick with a fork.

Poach the haddock in a saucepan with enough water to cover and half the lemon juice for about 5 minutes until tender. Drain, remove the skin and flake the fish with a fork. Melt the butter in a pan and sauté the mushrooms for 2 minutes. Combine them with the fish and spread evenly in the prepared flan case. Beat the eggs, add the milk, cottage cheese and remaining lemon juice and season well. Pour over the fish mixture.

Bake in the oven at 190°C (375°F) mark 5 for 45 minutes until set and golden.

Serves 6

Bacon and tomato hot pot

Illustrated in colour opposite

450-g (1-lb) lean bacon piece
450 g (1 lb) parsnips, trimmed and peeled
30 ml (2 level tbsp) plain wholemeal flour
30 ml (2 tbsp) chopped fresh parsley
freshly ground sea salt and pepper
2 medium onions, skinned and sliced
700 g (1$\frac{1}{2}$ lb) tomatoes, skinned and sliced
5 ml (1 level tsp) demerara sugar
150 ml ($\frac{1}{4}$ pint) chicken stock
50 g (2 oz) butter or vegetable margarine, melted

Cut the bacon into 1-cm ($\frac{1}{2}$-inch) cubes, removing any excess fat and skin. Place in a saucepan and cover with cold water. Bring to the boil, then drain. Thinly slice the parsnips and blanch in boiling water for 2 minutes, then drain well.

Mix the flour, parsley and seasonings together and toss the meat in the flour. Layer the meat, onions and tomatoes in a 1.7-litre (3-pint) ovenproof dish. Sprinkle with sugar and pour over the stock. Top with a layer of overlapping parsnip slices. Brush with the fat and bake in the oven at 180°C (350°F) mark 4 for 1$\frac{1}{4}$ hours, until tender. Serve with tomato sauce and fresh steamed vegetables sprinkled with toasted wholemeal croûtons (see page 76).

Serves 4

Bacon and tomato hot pot (*above*), Tomato sauce (*page 185*)

Stuffed green peppers with yogurt

2 medium green peppers
25 g (1 oz) butter
1 small onion, skinned and finely chopped
2 sticks of celery, trimmed, washed and chopped
50 g (2 oz) mushrooms, wiped and chopped
2.5 ml ($\frac{1}{2}$ level tsp) chopped fresh parsley
2.5 ml ($\frac{1}{2}$ level tsp) chopped fresh sage
15 ml (1 level tbsp) tomato purée
a dash of Worcestershire sauce
150 ml ($\frac{1}{4}$ pint) natural yogurt
freshly ground sea salt and pepper

Blanch the peppers in boiling water for a few minutes, drain, then cut them in half lengthways and discard the seeds. Place the peppers in an ovenproof dish.

Melt the butter in a frying pan and fry the onion, celery and mushrooms together for 3–4 minutes, until soft. Stir in the parsley, sage, tomato purée, Worcestershire sauce and yogurt, reserving 30 ml (2 tbsp) yogurt for the topping. Season well and fill the peppers with the mixture. Cover the dish with foil and bake in the oven at 190°C (375°F) mark 5 for about 35 minutes until the peppers are tender. Top each pepper half with the remaining yogurt and bake, uncovered, for a further 5–6 minutes. Serve with tomato sauce (see page 185).

Serves 4

Soused herrings

4 large or 6–8 small herrings, cleaned and boned
freshly ground sea salt and pepper
1 small onion, skinned and sliced
6 peppercorns
1–2 bay leaves
a few fresh parsley sprigs
150 ml ($\frac{1}{4}$ pint) malt vinegar
about 150 ml ($\frac{1}{4}$ pint) water

Trim the heads, tails and fins from the fish, remove any remaining bones and sprinkle with salt and pepper. Roll the fish up from the head end and secure with wooden cocktail sticks. Pack them into a fairly shallow ovenproof dish and add the onion, peppercorns and herbs. Pour in the vinegar and enough water to almost cover the fish. Cover with greaseproof paper or foil and bake in the oven at 180°C (350°F) mark 4 for about 45 minutes, until tender. Leave the herrings to cool in the cooking liquid before serving with a salad.

Serves 4

NOTE If you wish, the tails can be left on the fish. When packing the rolled fish into the dish, arrange the tails pointing upwards. Herrings can also be soused whole.

Cheese mousse

25 g (1 oz) powdered gelatine
225 g (8 oz) Cheddar cheese, grated
½ a small cucumber, washed and grated
1 garlic clove, skinned and crushed
400 ml (¾ pint) natural yogurt
15 ml (1 tbsp) mayonnaise (see page 171)
2.5 ml (½ level tsp) mustard powder
15 ml (1 level tbsp) chopped fresh parsley
freshly ground sea salt and pepper
watercress sprigs to garnish

Put 90 ml (6 tbsp) water in a small bowl and sprinkle in the gelatine. Stand the bowl over a pan of hot water and heat gently until the gelatine has dissolved. Mix together the cheese, cucumber, garlic, yogurt, mayonnaise, mustard, parsley, salt and pepper. Whisk in the gelatine mixture. Pour into a 600-ml (1-pint) ring mould and leave in a cool place until set. To serve, turn out and garnish with the watercress.

Serves 4–6

Lamb broth

700 g (1½ lb) scrag end neck of lamb, trimmed of fat
1.7 litres (3 pints) water
bouquet garni
5 ml (1 level tsp) chopped fresh thyme
3 large carrots, trimmed and peeled
50 g (2 oz) vegetable margarine
225 g (8 oz) leeks, trimmed, sliced and washed
1 large turnip, peeled and diced
1 small onion, skinned and chopped
2 sticks of celery, trimmed, washed and sliced
50 g (2 oz) pot barley
freshly ground sea salt and pepper

Place the lamb in a large saucepan, cover with cold water and bring to the boil. Drain, refresh under cold running water and drain again. Replace the meat in the pan and cover with the water. Add the bouquet garni, thyme and carrots and simmer, covered, for about 1 hour or until the meat is tender.

Melt the margarine in a large pan and stir in the leeks, turnip, onion and celery. Fry gently, covered, for 10 minutes or until lightly browned. Strain the lamb stock over the vegetables and simmer gently for a further 20 minutes. Strip the meat off the bones, slice the cooked carrots and add to the pan with the barley and seasoning. Simmer for about 40 minutes until all is tender. Serve with chunks of lightly buttered wholemeal bread.

Serves 4

Bean sprout salad

100 g (4 oz) mung bean sprouts
1 small onion, skinned and chopped
100 g (4 oz) cold cooked chicken, cut into strips
1 lettuce, washed
chopped fresh parsley to garnish

For the dressing
10 ml (2 level tsp) chopped fresh tarragon
5 ml (1 level tsp) mustard powder
30 ml (2 tbsp) olive oil
10 ml (2 tsp) tarragon vinegar

Wash and dry the bean sprouts and put them in a bowl with the onion and chicken. To make the dressing, whisk all the ingredients together until well blended, or put them in a screw-topped jar and shake vigorously. Pour over the bean sprout mixture and toss lightly together. Serve on a bed of lettuce, garnished with chopped parsley.

Serves 2

Tomato mould

225 ml (8 fl oz) chicken stock
50 g (2 oz) powdered gelatine
juice of 1 lemon
1 large onion, skinned and sliced
8 drops of Tabasco sauce
60 ml (4 tbsp) Worcestershire sauce
5 ml (1 level tsp) celery salt
900 ml ($1\frac{1}{2}$ pints) tomato juice

For the filling
75 g (3 oz) brown rice
2 tomatoes, skinned and chopped
50 ml (2 fl oz) French dressing (see page 172)

Pour the stock into a small bowl and sprinkle in the gelatine. Stand the bowl over a pan of hot water and heat gently until the gelatine has dissolved. Put the gelatine and stock and all the ingredients, except the filling ingredients, into a blender and blend them at high speed for about 30 seconds or until smooth. Rinse a 1.1-litre (2-pint) ring mould with cold water, then pour in the tomato mixture and chill for 1–2 hours, or until set.

For the filling, bring a saucepan of lightly salted water to the boil. Stir in the rice, cover and simmer for 40–45 minutes, or until the rice is just tender. Drain, rinse in cold water to stop the cooking process and drain again. Stir in the tomatoes and French dressing and chill. To serve, turn out the tomato mould on to a plate and fill the centre with the rice mixture.

Serves 4

Stuffed jacket potatoes

4 large potatoes, scrubbed
30 ml (2 tbsp) milk
25 g (1 oz) butter
freshly ground sea salt and pepper

Prick the potatoes with a fork and bake them in the oven at 200°C (400°F) mark 6 for $1-1\frac{1}{2}$ hours or until soft when squeezed. Break open or cut a slice from the top and scoop out the flesh into a warmed bowl. Cream with milk and butter and season well. Mix the creamed potato with any of the following fillings and pile into the empty potato jackets to serve.

Filling 1
175 g (6 oz) Cheddar cheese, grated
60 ml (4 level tbsp) chutney

Filling 2
450 g (1 lb) minced beef, cooked
1 small onion, skinned and finely chopped

Filling 3
225 g (8 oz) lean ham, finely chopped
30 ml (2 level tbsp) pickle

Filling 4
175 g (6 oz) curd cheese or cottage
cheese, sieved
or 150 ml ($\frac{1}{4}$ pint) natural yogurt
20 ml (4 level tsp) chopped fresh chives

Filling 5
1 stick of celery, trimmed, washed and
finely chopped
100 g (4 oz) Red Leicester cheese, grated
25 g (1 oz) walnuts, roughly chopped

Filling 6
100 g (4 oz) lean unsmoked bacon, grilled
and finely chopped
2 spring onions, finely chopped
50 g (2 oz) peanuts
60 ml (4 tbsp) soured cream

Serves 4

Cheesy eggs

25 g (1 oz) butter
100 g (4 oz) mushrooms, wiped and sliced
freshly ground sea salt and pepper
4 hard-boiled eggs
225 g (8 oz) Cheddar cheese, thinly sliced or grated

Melt the butter in a pan and lightly fry the mushrooms for 5 minutes or until soft. Season with salt and pepper. Place the hard-boiled eggs in a flameproof dish, spoon over the mushrooms and cover with cheese. Grill until the cheese melts.

Serves 4

Cottage cheese and ham cocottes

40 g (1½ oz) butter
1 small onion, skinned and finely chopped
225 g (8 oz) cottage cheese, sieved
2 eggs
1 slice of ham, trimmed of fat and chopped
100 g (4 oz) button mushrooms, wiped and sliced
freshly ground sea salt and pepper
30 ml (2 level tbsp) chopped fresh parsley, chervil or tarragon
50 g (2 oz) Cheddar cheese, grated

Melt 15 g (½ oz) butter in a pan and fry the onion for 5 minutes, until soft, then drain. Melt the remaining butter in another pan and use to brush four individual ovenproof dishes or cocottes. Place them on a baking sheet. Beat the cottage cheese and eggs together. Stir in the ham, mushrooms and onion, then season to taste. Mix in half the chopped herbs. Divide the mixture between the four dishes and sprinkle with grated cheese. Bake in the oven at 200°C (400°F) mark 6 for 10–15 minutes until golden. Garnish with the remaining herbs and serve immediately.

Serves 4

Pumpernickel snack

4 slices of pumpernickel bread
butter or vegetable margarine
1 lettuce, washed
100 g (4 oz) curd cheese
30 ml (2 tbsp) natural yogurt
4 silver skin (cocktail) onions, finely chopped
2 small gherkins, finely chopped
50 g (2 oz) lean ham, finely diced
freshly ground sea salt and pepper
1 tomato, sliced, and 4 walnut halves to garnish

Spread the slices of pumpernickel with a little butter or margarine. Place a lettuce leaf on each slice of bread. Cream the curd cheese with the yogurt until smooth and add the onion, gherkin, ham and seasoning. Spoon on to the centre of each lettuce leaf and garnish with a slice of tomato and a walnut half.

Serves 4

Herring roes on toast

15 ml (1 level tbsp) plain wholemeal flour
freshly ground sea salt and pepper
450 g (1 lb) herring roes, washed
25 g (1 oz) butter, melted
4 slices of wholemeal bread, toasted and lightly buttered
cayenne pepper (optional)
1 lemon, cut into wedges

Line a grill pan with greased foil. Season the flour with salt and pepper and dip the roes in the flour. Brush them over with melted butter and arrange them in the grill pan. Cook under a moderately hot grill for 8–10 minutes, tossing occasionally, until evenly cooked and tender. Serve on hot toast, sprinkled with cayenne pepper if liked, and accompanied by a wedge of lemon.

Serves 4

Chinese rice

225 g (8 oz) brown rice
60 ml (4 tbsp) groundnut or sunflower oil
freshly ground sea salt and pepper
3 eggs, beaten
225 g (8 oz) peeled shrimps
100 g (4 oz) mushrooms, wiped and sliced
100 g (4 oz) cold cooked chicken, cut into strips
100 g (4 oz) cold cooked pork, trimmed of fat and diced
60 ml (4 tbsp) chicken stock
30 ml (2 tbsp) Marsala
15 ml (1 tbsp) tamari sauce
chopped fresh parsley to garnish

Bring a saucepan of lightly salted water to the boil. Stir in the rice, cover and simmer for 40–45 minutes or until the rice is just tender. Drain, rinse in cold water to stop the cooking process and drain again.

Heat 15 ml (1 tbsp) oil in a small frying pan, tilting the pan so that the surface is evenly greased. Season the beaten eggs well, pour into the pan and heat gently. Stir with a fork, allowing the uncooked egg to run to the sides of the pan to cook. Once the egg has set, stop stirring and cook until the under-side of the omelette is golden brown. Remove from the pan and drain well. Cut into long strips and keep warm.

Heat a further 30 ml (2 tbsp) oil and fry the shrimps lightly. Add the mushrooms, chicken and pork. Heat through well, remove from the pan, drain and keep hot with the egg strips. Heat the remaining oil, add the rice and stir over a low heat. Add the stock, Marsala, tamari sauce and season well. Add all the other ingredients to the pan and heat through. Pile on to a hot serving dish, garnish with parsley and serve immediately.

Serves 4

Courgettes provençale

25 g (1 oz) butter
1 shallot or small onion, skinned and chopped
1 garlic clove, skinned and finely chopped
6 courgettes, trimmed and thickly sliced
450 g (1 lb) tomatoes, skinned and sliced
100 g (4 oz) Cheddar cheese, grated
freshly ground sea salt and pepper

Heat the butter and gently fry the shallot or onion and garlic for 2 minutes, until soft. Add the courgettes and sauté for 10 minutes, turning frequently, until tender. Add the tomatoes and cook for a few minutes more, until the tomatoes are slightly pulpy. Arrange the sautéed vegetables in layers with the grated cheese in an ovenproof dish, seasoning each vegetable layer with salt and pepper and finishing with a layer of cheese.

Cook in the oven at 180°C (350°F) mark 4 for 30–40 minutes until the top is golden.

Serves 4

Salade niçoise

225 g (8 oz) tomatoes, skinned and sliced
$\frac{1}{2}$ a small cucumber, thinly sliced
freshly ground sea salt and pepper
5 ml (1 level tsp) chopped fresh basil
5 ml (1 level tsp) chopped fresh parsley
grated rind of 1 lemon
100 g (4 oz) cooked French beans
50 g (2 oz) black olives, stoned and chopped
8 anchovy fillets, halved
1 lemon, quartered, to garnish

For the dressing
60 ml (4 tbsp) olive oil
30 ml (2 tbsp) cider vinegar
1 garlic clove, skinned and crushed
freshly ground sea salt and pepper

Put the tomatoes and cucumber in layers in a shallow dish, season well and sprinkle with the herbs and lemon rind. Pile the French beans in the centre of the dish, scatter the olives over and season again.

To make the dressing, whisk all the ingredients together until well blended, or put all the ingredients in a screw-topped jar and shake vigorously. Pour over the salad. Arrange the anchovy fillets in a lattice pattern over the salad and leave for about 30 minutes before serving to allow the flavours to blend.

Serve garnished with the lemon quarters and accompanied by slices of wholemeal bread and butter.

Serves 4

Tomato toasts

25 g (1 oz) butter
25 g (1 oz) plain wholemeal flour
300 ml ($\frac{1}{2}$ pint) milk
75 g (3 oz) Cheddar cheese, grated
freshly ground sea salt and pepper
4 large tomatoes
4 slices of wholemeal bread, toasted and lightly buttered
chopped fresh parsley to garnish

Melt the butter in a saucepan, add the flour and cook for 1–2 minutes. Remove from the heat and gradually stir in the milk. Return to the heat and cook slowly, stirring continuously, until the sauce boils and thickens. Cook for 2–3 minutes. Add the cheese and seasoning and cook until the cheese has melted. Slice the tomatoes in half and grill. Place the tomato halves on the toast and coat with sauce. Serve sprinkled with parsley.

Serves 2

Baked stuffed onions

4 medium onions, skinned
30 ml (2 level tbsp) fresh wholemeal breadcrumbs
freshly ground sea salt and pepper
50 g (2 oz) Cheddar cheese, grated
a little milk
a little butter

For the sauce
25 g (1 oz) butter
25 g (1 oz) plain wholemeal flour
400 ml ($\frac{3}{4}$ pint) milk
50 g (2 oz) Cheddar cheese, grated
freshly ground sea salt and pepper

Cook the onions in boiling salted water for 15–20 minutes, removing them before they are soft. Drain and leave to cool. Cut the tops off the onions, using a sharp, pointed knife, and scoop out the centres with a teaspoon. Chop the onion centres finely, mix with the breadcrumbs, seasoning and half the cheese, and moisten with a little milk if necessary. Fill the onions with this mixture and place them in a greased ovenproof dish. Put small knobs of butter on top and sprinkle with the remaining grated cheese. Bake in the oven at 200°C (400°F) mark 6 for 20–30 minutes until the onions are cooked and brown.

To make the sauce, melt the butter in a saucepan and stir in the flour. Cook for 1–2 minutes. Remove from the heat and gradually stir in the milk. If liked, use some of the onion liquor and make up to 400 ml ($\frac{3}{4}$ pint) with milk. Bring to the boil, stirring all the time, until the sauce thickens. Stir in the cheese, salt and pepper and cook until the cheese has melted. Serve the sauce with the onions.

Serves 4

Mushroom omelette

2 eggs
freshly ground sea salt and pepper
15 g ($\frac{1}{2}$ oz) butter

For the filling
15 g ($\frac{1}{2}$ oz) butter
50 g (2 oz) mushrooms, wiped and sliced
5 ml (1 level tsp) chopped fresh chives

Lightly whisk the eggs, seasoning and 15 ml (1 tbsp) water together. Melt the butter in a frying pan over a medium heat, tilting the pan so that the surface is evenly greased. Pour in the egg mixture and gently stir with a fork, allowing the uncooked egg to flow to the sides and cook. Once the egg has set, stop stirring and cook the omelette for another minute, until the under-side is golden brown.

For the filling, melt the butter and lightly fry the mushrooms for about 3 minutes until tender. Stir in the chopped chives. Spoon the filling on to the centre of the omelette and, using a palette knife, fold the omelette by flicking one third over to the centre, then fold over the opposite side. Turn the omelette on to a warmed plate, folded side underneath, and serve immediately.

Serves 1

Mexican beans

225 g (8 oz) red kidney beans, soaked (see page 23)
4 sticks of celery, trimmed, washed and chopped
25 g (1 oz) gherkins, chopped
1 small onion, skinned and finely chopped
1 lettuce, washed
a few celery leaves to garnish

For the dressing
60 ml (4 tbsp) sunflower oil
30 ml (2 tbsp) malt vinegar
pinch of chilli powder
2.5 ml ($\frac{1}{2}$ level tsp) French mustard
1.25 ml ($\frac{1}{4}$ level tsp) demerara sugar
freshly ground sea salt and pepper

Drain the kidney beans and cook in boiling water for about 1 hour, until tender. Drain well, then place in a mixing bowl. Place the oil, vinegar, chilli powder, mustard, sugar, salt and pepper in a screw-topped jar. Shake well, pour over the beans and toss together. Leave to cool. Add the celery, gherkins and onion. Arrange the lettuce in a serving bowl and pile the bean mixture on top, spooning over any remaining dressing. Garnish with celery leaves.

Serves 4

Cheesy topped salad rolls

4 wholemeal rolls
butter or vegetable margarine
50 g (2 oz) white cabbage, trimmed and finely shredded
1 stick of celery, trimmed, washed and finely chopped
1 small eating apple, cored and finely chopped
5 ml (1 tsp) lemon juice
45 ml (3 tbsp) mayonnaise (see page 171)
50 g (2 oz) Red Leicester cheese, grated

Cut the rolls in half and spread with a little butter or margarine. Mix the cabbage, celery, apple, lemon juice and mayonnaise together and spoon the filling on to the bottom halves of the rolls. Sandwich together with the tops of the rolls and sprinkle with grated cheese. Put under a hot grill for about 1 minute, until the cheese has melted.

Serves 4

Eggs in baked potatoes

4 large potatoes, scrubbed
25 g (1 oz) butter
freshly ground sea salt and pepper
30 ml (2 tbsp) milk
4 eggs

Prick the potatoes with a fork and bake them in the oven at 200°C (400°F) mark 6 for $1-1\frac{1}{2}$ hours, until slightly soft when squeezed.

Break open the potatoes or cut a slice from the top and scoop out the flesh into a warmed bowl. Cream with the butter, seasoning and milk. Half-fill each potato case with the mixture, break an egg in on top and return to the oven for 10–15 minutes, until the eggs are set. Pipe the remaining potato round the top and brown under the grill.

Serves 4

Mixed bean salad

275 g (10 oz) mixed dried beans, *eg.* aduki,
red kidney, black, haricots, soaked (see page 23)
100 ml (4 fl oz) French dressing (see page 172)
2.5 ml ($\frac{1}{2}$ level tsp) ground coriander
1 small onion, skinned and finely sliced
freshly ground sea salt and pepper

Drain the beans and cook in boiling water for about 1 hour until tender. (If aduki beans are included, add them half-way through the cooking time.)

Drain the beans and place in a large salad bowl. Combine the French dressing and coriander and pour over the beans while they are still warm. Toss thoroughly and leave to cool. Mix the onion into the beans, season and chill before serving.

Serves 4

Onion and cheese pie

2 medium onions, skinned and chopped
100 g (4 oz) Cheddar cheese, grated
30 ml (2 tbsp) natural yogurt
1 egg, beaten
freshly ground sea salt and pepper
275 g (10 oz) wholemeal pastry (see page 237)

Cook the onions in boiling salted water for 5 minutes until soft, then drain. Mix with the cheese and yogurt, add nearly all the beaten egg and season to taste.

Roll out half the pastry on a lightly floured surface and use to line an 18-cm (7-inch) pie plate. Pour the cheese mixture into the centre. Roll out the remaining pastry to form a lid. Dampen the edges of the pastry on the plate with water and cover with the lid, pressing the edges well together. Flake and scallop the edge and brush with the remaining beaten egg. Bake in the oven at 200°C (400°F) mark 6 for about 30 minutes, until the pastry is golden brown.

Serves 4

Salad lunch

1 stick of celery, trimmed, washed and chopped
$\frac{1}{2}$ a green pepper, seeded and sliced
5-cm (2-inch) piece of cucumber, sliced
1 eating apple, cored and sliced
15 g ($\frac{1}{2}$ oz) walnuts, chopped
25 g (1 oz) seedless raisins

For the dressing
10 ml (2 tsp) lemon juice
freshly ground sea salt and pepper
60 ml (4 tbsp) natural yogurt

Mix the celery, pepper, cucumber, apple, walnuts and raisins together. Make the dressing by whisking all the ingredients together until well blended. Pour the dressing over the salad and toss well just before serving.

Serves 2

Cheese soufflé omelette

7 g ($\frac{1}{4}$ oz) butter
1 egg, size 2, separated
freshly ground sea salt and pepper
25 g (1 oz) Cheddar cheese, grated

Melt the butter in a small frying pan, then whisk the egg white until stiff. In a separate bowl, beat the egg yolk, seasoning and 15 ml (1 tbsp) cold water together until mixed. Fold the egg white into the yolk mixture and pour into the pan. Cook over a low heat until the under-side is set and lightly browned, then sprinkle with the cheese and place under a hot grill until the cheese has melted. Fold the omelette in half and turn on to a warmed serving dish. Serve immediately, accompanied by a crisp salad.

Serves 1

Chicken rice salad

1 eating apple, halved and cored
juice of $\frac{1}{2}$ a lemon
225 g (8 oz) cold cooked chicken, chopped
50 g (2 oz) brown rice, cooked
1 celery heart, trimmed, washed and diced
25 g (1 oz) seedless raisins
1 hard-boiled egg, chopped
a little mayonnaise (see page 171)
freshly ground sea salt and pepper

Dice the apple and toss in a little lemon juice. Mix the chicken, rice, celery and apple. Add the raisins and egg, mix with enough mayonnaise to bind and add a little seasoning. Serve in a large bowl or in individual portions on crisp lettuce leaves, with other salad vegetables, such as chicory and radishes, if liked.

Serves 2

Tahitian salad

1 lettuce, washed
4 slices of fresh pineapple or
2 bananas, peeled and halved lengthways
450 g (1 lb) curd cheese or cottage cheese, sieved
chopped fresh chives
grated coconut

Arrange the lettuce on a plate, place the pineapple slices or banana halves on it and divide the cheese evenly between them. Sprinkle with chives and coconut.

Serves 4

NOTE If using bananas, dip the pieces in lemon juice before arranging them on the plate to prevent discoloration.

Wholemeal sandwiches

Make up any of the following sandwich fillings by simply combining the ingredients, to make tasty wholemeal sandwiches.

Soft cheese, celery and pimiento
75 g (3 oz) curd cheese or cottage cheese
1 stick of celery, washed and chopped
30 ml (2 level tbsp) chopped red pimiento
freshly ground sea salt and pepper
Makes sufficient for 4 rounds

Soft cheese, walnut and raisins
100 g (4 oz) curd cheese or cottage cheese
25 g (1 oz) walnuts, chopped
20 ml (4 level tsp) seedless raisins
freshly ground sea salt and pepper
Makes sufficient for 3 rounds

Crab and avocado
100 g (4 oz) crab meat, flaked
25 g (1 oz) avocado flesh, mashed
60 ml (4 tbsp) mayonnaise (see page 171)
freshly ground sea salt and pepper
Makes sufficient for 4 rounds

Tuna fish and tomato
200-g (7-oz) can tuna fish, drained and flaked
2 large tomatoes, chopped
60 ml (4 tbsp) mayonnaise (see page 171)
freshly ground sea salt and pepper
Makes sufficient for 5 rounds

Red Leicester and tomato
225 g (8 oz) Red Leicester cheese, grated
4 small tomatoes, chopped
30 ml (2 level tbsp) tomato purée
Makes sufficient for 4 rounds

Cheshire and Worcestershire sauce
225 g (8 oz) Cheshire cheese, grated
30 ml (2 tbsp) Worcestershire sauce
30 ml (2 level tbsp) tomato purée
Makes sufficient for 4 rounds

Lancashire and sultana
225 g (8 oz) Lancashire cheese, grated
50 g (2 oz) sultanas
45 ml (3 tbsp) white wine vinegar
Makes sufficient for 4 rounds

Wensleydale and date
225 g (8 oz) Wensleydale cheese, grated
7.5 ml ($1\frac{1}{2}$ level tsp) English mustard
40 g ($1\frac{1}{2}$ oz) pressed dates, finely chopped
Makes sufficient for 4 rounds

Peanut butter
225 g (8 oz) peanuts, shelled
30 ml (2 tbsp) groundnut oil
pinch of freshly ground sea salt

Put the peanuts in a single layer on a baking sheet with low sides. Bake in the oven at 150°C (300°F) mark 2 for 20 minutes until browned. Transfer immediately to a cold plate. Rub off all the skins, either individually with your fingers or by putting them into a clean tea towel or polythene bag and rubbing them together. Put the skinned nuts into a blender and blend until finely ground but quite dry. Add the oil and blend again to obtain a glossy paste. Taste and add salt if necessary.

Makes about 225 g (8 oz)

Carrot and cottage cheese salad

450 g (1 lb) cottage cheese
350 g (12 oz) carrots, trimmed, peeled and grated
25 g (1 oz) currants
60 ml (4 tbsp) mayonnaise (see page 171)
10 ml (2 tsp) lemon juice
freshly ground sea salt and pepper
1 lettuce, washed and shredded

Mix the cottage cheese, carrots and currants together. Blend with the mayonnaise and lemon juice and season well with salt and pepper. Serve on a bed of shredded lettuce.

Serves 4

Brown rice salad

225 g (8 oz) brown rice
60 ml (4 tbsp) olive or sunflower oil
juice of 1 lemon
75 g (3 oz) Cheddar cheese, grated
50 g (2 oz) peanuts
100 g (4 oz) mushrooms, wiped and sliced
1 large green pepper, seeded and finely chopped
50 g (2 oz) mung bean sprouts

Bring a saucepan of lightly salted water to the boil. Stir in the rice, cover and simmer for 40–45 minutes, or until the rice is just tender. Drain, rinse in cold water to stop the cooking process and drain again.

Put the rice in a bowl and mix in the oil and lemon juice. Stir in the cheese and peanuts with a fork. Finally, add the mushrooms, pepper and bean sprouts.

Serves 4

Herrings in oatmeal

4 herrings, cleaned and heads and tails removed
freshly ground sea salt and pepper
100 g (4 oz) fine oatmeal
$\frac{1}{2}$ a lemon, cut into wedges and chopped fresh parsley to garnish

Slit the fish along the under-side. Open out each fish, place cut-side-down on a board and press down firmly on the backbone to flatten. Turn the fish over and remove the backbone. Rub the fish with a little salt, rinse and dry well. Sprinkle with salt and pepper and coat with oatmeal, pressing it well into the fish on both sides.

Line a grill pan with foil and pre-heat until fairly hot. Arrange the herrings in the pan and grill, turning carefully, for 6–8 minutes or until tender and slightly flaky. Serve garnished with lemon wedges and chopped parsley.

Serves 4

Winter vegetable and barley soup

30 ml (2 tbsp) sunflower oil
1 large onion, skinned and chopped
2 carrots, trimmed, peeled and finely diced
2 leeks, trimmed, sliced and washed
1 medium swede, peeled and finely diced
1 turnip, peeled and finely diced
2 sticks of celery, trimmed, washed and sliced
900 ml (1½ pints) chicken stock
300 ml (½ pint) tomato juice
25 g (1 oz) pot barley
freshly ground sea salt and pepper
15 ml (1 tbsp) Worcestershire sauce

Heat the oil in a large saucepan and fry the vegetables for about 5 minutes, until soft. Add the remaining ingredients and bring to the boil. Cover and simmer gently for about 1 hour, until all the vegetables are tender and the pot barley is cooked. Serve with hot wholemeal rolls.

Serves 4–6

Peanut basted chicken

Illustrated in colour opposite

4 chicken leg portions
75 g (3 oz) peanuts, roasted
140 g (5½ oz) butter or vegetable margarine
10 ml (2 level tsp) ground cumin
freshly ground sea salt and pepper
4 onion slices
4 small peaches, halved and stoned
chopped fresh parsley to garnish

Divide each leg portion into two and remove the knobbly leg ends. Roughly chop half the nuts and grind the remainder in a blender. Beat all the nuts into 75 g (3 oz) of the fat with the cumin, salt and pepper.

Line a grill pan with foil and arrange the chicken portions, skin-side down, in the pan. Spread a little of the nut mixture over the chicken, arrange the onion slices in the pan and dot with half the remaining fat. Grill gently for 10–15 minutes, roughing up the mixture on the portions with a fork from time to time to prevent burning. Turn the chicken over, spread with the remaining nut mixture, add the peach halves to the pan and dot with fat. Grill for a further 12–15 minutes until the chicken is tender.

Serve the chicken topped with onion rings and parsley, with the grilled peach halves alongside.

Serves 4

Vegetable curry with eggs

Illustrated in colour opposite

225 g (8 oz) aubergine, trimmed and cubed
freshly ground sea salt
1 small cauliflower, trimmed
450 g (1 lb) courgettes, trimmed and sliced
50 g (2 oz) butter or vegetable margarine
2 medium onions, skinned and chopped
30 ml (2 level tbsp) curry paste
40 g ($1\frac{1}{2}$ oz) plain wholemeal flour
300 ml ($\frac{1}{2}$ pint) chicken stock
150 ml ($\frac{1}{4}$ pint) tomato juice
4 tomatoes, skinned and chopped
50 g (2 oz) cashew nuts
50 g (2 oz) Cheddar cheese, grated
grated rind of 1 small lemon
6 eggs
chopped fresh parsley to garnish

Sprinkle the aubergine with salt, leave for about 30 minutes, then rinse well and pat dry. Cut the cauliflower into florets and blanch in boiling, salted water for 5 minutes. Drain, then blanch the courgettes in the same water for 4 minutes, then drain.

Melt the fat in a frying pan and fry the onion and aubergine for 5–10 minutes, until lightly browned. Stir in the curry paste and flour and cook for 1 minute, then stir in the chicken stock and tomato juice. Cook for a few minutes more, stirring, until thickened.

Place the cauliflower, courgettes and tomatoes in a large ovenproof dish and pour the aubergine mixture over. Combine the nuts, cheese and lemon rind and sprinkle over the centre. Bake in the oven at 190°C (375°F) mark 5 for about 25 minutes.

Meanwhile, cook the eggs, timed to be ready at the same time as the curry. Place them in cold water, bring to the boil and cook for 8 minutes. When the curry is ready, spoon on to a heated serving dish. Shell, halve and arrange the hot eggs round the curry and garnish with chopped parsley.

Serves 4

Leek pancakes

225 g (8 oz) plain wholemeal flour
5 ml (1 level tsp) baking powder
pinch of freshly ground sea salt
2 eggs, beaten
300 ml ($\frac{1}{2}$ pint) milk and water, mixed
a little sunflower oil
watercress to garnish

For the filling
900 g (2 lb) leeks, trimmed, thickly sliced and washed
25 g (1 oz) butter
25 g (1 oz) plain wholemeal flour
300 ml ($\frac{1}{2}$ pint) milk
75 g (3 oz) Cheddar cheese, grated
freshly ground sea salt and pepper

Make a pancake batter by mixing the flour, baking powder and salt together in a bowl. Make a well in the centre and pour in the beaten eggs. Pour in some of the milk and water and beat all together. Add the rest of the liquid and beat until the batter is well mixed and smooth.

For the filling, cook the leeks in boiling salted water for 5–8 minutes, until tender but still firm. Drain well. Melt the butter in a saucepan, add the flour and cook for 1–2 minutes. Remove from the heat and gradually add the milk. Return to the heat and cook, stirring, until boiling and thickened. Simmer for 2 minutes. Add the cheese to the sauce, stirring in well until melted. Remove from the heat, season and add the leeks.

Make the pancakes by heating a little oil in an 18-cm (7-inch) frying pan until hot, tilting the pan so that the surface is evenly oiled. Pour off any surplus. Pour a little batter into the pan, moving the pan to and fro until the base is covered. Cook over a medium heat until the under-side of the pancake is golden brown. Turn it with a palette knife or by tossing and cook the second side until golden. Repeat, lightly oiling the pan each time, until eight pancakes are made. Keep the pancakes hot on a plate in a warm oven. Divide the warm filling between the pancakes. Roll up and place on a large heated serving dish. Serve hot, garnished with watercress.

Serves 4

Spinach roulade

900 g (2 lb) spinach, trimmed and washed
freshly ground sea salt and pepper
4 eggs, size 2, separated
100 g (4 oz) curd cheese
30 ml (2 tbsp) natural yogurt

Grease and line a 35.5 × 25.5-cm (14 × 10-inch) Swiss roll tin. Coarsely chop the spinach, pack it wet into a saucepan and season with salt and pepper. Cook gently, covered, for about 10 minutes until tender, then drain well. Allow to cool slightly, then beat in the egg yolks. Whisk the egg whites until stiff then fold into the spinach mixture. Spread the mixture in the prepared tin and bake in the oven at 200°C (400°F) mark 6 for about 20 minutes, until firm. Meanwhile, beat the cheese and yogurt together.

When the roulade is cooked, turn it out on to greaseproof paper, peel off the lining paper and spread immediately and quickly with the cheese mixture. Roll the roulade up by gently lifting the greaseproof paper. Serve hot or cold, cut into thick slices, with wholemeal bread and butter.

Serves 4

Avocado and grapefruit salad

Illustrated in colour on page 51

2 medium grapefruit
225 g (8 oz) Cheddar cheese
150 ml ($\frac{1}{4}$ pint) soured cream
freshly ground sea salt and pepper
3 large ripe avocados
25 g (1 oz) cashew nuts, toasted
paprika to garnish
1 lettuce, washed

Cut all the skin and pith away from the grapefruit using a serrated knife. Do this over a bowl to catch the juice. Divide the flesh into segments. Slice the cheese into thin strips and mix with the grapefruit, grapefruit juice, soured cream and seasoning.

Halve the avocados, remove the stones and pile the salad mixture into the centre of each one. Sprinkle the cashew nuts over the avocados and dust lightly with paprika.

Arrange the lettuce leaves on individual serving plates and serve the avocados on top.

Serves 6

Cottage cheese stuffed tomatoes

4 large firm tomatoes
100 g (4 oz) cottage cheese
15 ml (1 level tbsp) chopped onion
25 g (1 oz) sultanas
freshly ground sea salt and pepper
pinch of ground ginger

Cut a slice off the end of each tomato and scoop out the flesh. Combine the tomato with all the other ingredients and use to stuff the tomato cases. Replace the tops.

Serves 4

All-in-one slimming salad

450 g (1 lb) cottage cheese
30 ml (2 level tbsp) tomato purée
1 garlic clove, skinned and crushed (optional)
225 g (8 oz) tomatoes, chopped
1 small red pepper, seeded and chopped
1 bunch of watercress, finely chopped
1 large carrot, trimmed, peeled and grated
freshly ground sea salt and pepper
25 g (1 oz) sprouted alfalfa
50 g (2 oz) seedless raisins

Put the cottage cheese into a bowl and mix in the tomato purée and garlic, if used. Stir until well incorporated, then add the remaining ingredients.

Serves 4

Kidney sauté

25 g (1 oz) vegetable margarine
1 medium onion, skinned and chopped
100 g (4 oz) button mushrooms, wiped and sliced
450 g (1 lb) lambs' kidneys, skinned and cored
15 ml (1 level tbsp) tomato purée
freshly ground sea salt and pepper
15 ml (1 tbsp) lemon juice
60 ml (4 tbsp) soured cream
chopped fresh parsley to garnish

Melt the margarine in a saucepan and fry the onion for 5 minutes until soft. Add the mushrooms and cook for a further 2–3 minutes. Cut the kidneys into pieces and add to the pan with the tomato purée, seasoning and lemon juice. Cook for 5–6 minutes until browned, remove from the heat and stir in the soured cream. Serve sprinkled with chopped parsley and accompanied by boiled brown rice.

Serves 4

Soups
and Starters

A soup or starter is the accepted thing when you are entertaining, but to many people it may seem extravagant or over-indulgent to serve them for family meals, especially wholefood ones where over-eating is not to be encouraged. However, when you come to consider it, you will find what a good idea they are, both economically and nutritionally.

If you all sit down to the table ravenously hungry and eat the main course straight away, you will probably eat far more than if you had had something else, however small, to begin with. And you might well have plenty of room left at the end for a heavy and fattening sweet.

A small but delectable first course can also help when anyone is not feeling hungry enough for the main course. It will tempt their palate and work up an appetite. It will also get people in the mood for eating and help them relax while waiting for the main part of the meal, and it is generally felt that the more happy and relaxed you feel, the more goodness you will derive from your food.

Starters

First courses can be based on fruit, vegetables or small amounts of protein foods such as eggs, cheese, fish or pulses. Fruit can be simple, such as a cut grapefruit or a slice of melon topped with grapes. You can also top fruit with curd or cream cheese or mix it into small and attractive salads.

Various dips such as a creamy cheese one or avocado-based Guacamole (see page 93) can be fun if you surround them with sticks of freshly cut vegetables called crudités. You can even make dips from pulses like the rich Hummus made from chick peas and sesame paste (see page 79). These are best served with wholemeal bread.

Small salads make ideal first courses and there are three ways of preparing them. You can either mix a small, leafy salad into a dressing and top it with a protein food; or you can leave the base plain, mix the protein part with a creamy dressing and spoon it over the top; or you can simply mix everything together. Small portions of lightly cooked fish or shellfish make ideal starters, but you may want to keep these for special occasions.

Soups

Soups are full of goodness and can be very cheap. You can have thick, warming ones in the winter and light-textured ones that can be chilled in the summer. Soups always taste far better and are more nutritious if you can make your own stock. To do this, buy a marrow bone, a chicken carcass or a set of giblets, or even a chicken portion. Put it into a large saucepan with a roughly chopped onion, carrot and stick of celery and set them on a low heat, without any fat, until they begin to brown. Top the saucepan up with cold water and put in a bouquet garni and 10 ml (2 level tsp) black peppercorns. Bring the water to the boil and simmer, uncovered, for $1\frac{1}{2}$ hours. Then strain off the liquid. The stock, when cool, can be poured into a plastic container, covered and stored in the refrigerator for up to a week.

Garnishes for soups

Every soup, no matter how humble, can be transformed into something special by the addition of garnishes. They can 'dress up' the appearance of the dish but they will also complement and enhance the flavour of the ingredients. Here are some suggestions:

WHOLEMEAL CROÛTONS go well with almost every type of soup – in fact with almost every type of dish (they taste particularly good in mixed salads, for instance). Try some scattered over creamed vegetable soups, such as watercress, and cold soups such as gazpacho. To make wholemeal croûtons, toast slices of wholemeal bread and cut them into small cubes.

YOGURT OR SOURED CREAM goes well with strong-flavoured soups such as bortsch. When using yogurt or soured cream as a flavouring in this way, do not add to the soup during cooking. Just before serving, either swirl into a tureen or spoon over the top of individual servings.

GRATED CHEESE makes an excellent addition to hearty vegetable, rice and pasta-based soups. The type of cheese depends on the flavour of the soup. The most usual ones are Cheddar and Parmesan but other cheeses such as Gruyère, Cheshire and Double Gloucester are just as good. For Italian-type soups, such as minestrone, grated Parmesan is probably most appropriate; for soups such as Scotch broth, vegetable and rice, use Cheddar or one of the other English cheeses; and for special soups, such as French onion soup, the best cheese to use would be Gruyère, if available.

JULIENNE VEGETABLES are vegetables cut into very slender sticks. They are the traditional accompaniment to consommés but they make an attractive addition to any clear broth-type soup. Root vegetables such as carrot, parsnip and celery are the most suitable but green peppers are also used sometimes.

FRESH HERBS Probably the most popular garnish of all and, depending on the herb, suitable for virtually all dishes. There are some standard pairings, though – tomato soups with basil; chicken soups with tarragon or rosemary; bean soups with savory; pea and ham soups with sage; potato and leek soups with chives. The list is endless and trying new combinations can be fun. Don't neglect the more esoteric herbs and spices for special effects – dill seed on potato soups; saffron or marigold leaves to lend both exotic colour and taste to fish soups.

Apricot, tomato and almond salad

6 apricots
6 tomatoes (about the same size as the apricots)
16 blanched almonds

For the dressing
60 ml (4 tbsp) soured cream
juice of $\frac{1}{2}$ a lemon
10 ml (2 tsp) clear honey
1 garlic clove, skinned and crushed
freshly ground sea salt and pepper

Halve and stone the apricots and cut them lengthways into thin slices. Cut the tomatoes in the same way and divide them both between four small bowls. Whisk the soured cream, lemon juice, honey, garlic and seasoning together until well blended and spoon over the apricots and tomatoes. Top with the almonds.

Serves 4

Tomato appetisers

100 g (4 oz) cucumber, peeled and diced
freshly ground sea salt and pepper
100 g (4 oz) curd cheese or cottage cheese, sieved
2.5 ml ($\frac{1}{2}$ level tsp) curry powder
4 large tomatoes
chopped fresh parsley to garnish

Sprinkle the cucumber with salt and leave for 30 minutes. Rinse off the salt and drain well. Cream the cheese until soft, add the cucumber and curry powder and season well. Cut the tops off the tomatoes, scoop out the centres and fill with the cheese mixture. Replace the tops and garnish with chopped parsley.

Serves 4

Melon, ginger and curd cheese salad

1 large, ripe honeydew melon
175 g (6 oz) curd cheese
5 ml (1 level tsp) ground ginger
1 garlic clove, skinned and crushed
freshly ground sea salt and pepper
15 ml (1 level tbsp) chopped fresh mint
8 mint leaves to garnish

Cut the melon lengthways into four and scoop out the seeds. Put the cheese into a bowl and work in the ginger, garlic, seasoning and chopped mint. Pile the cheese mixture into the centres of the melon pieces and garnish with the mint leaves.

Serves 4

Walnut-filled avocados

1 medium onion, skinned
$\frac{1}{2}$ a green pepper, seeded
1 bunch of radishes, trimmed
150 ml ($\frac{1}{4}$ pint) natural yogurt
25 g (1 oz) walnuts, chopped
15 ml (1 level tbsp) chopped fresh parsley
15 ml (1 level tbsp) chopped fresh chives
freshly ground sea salt and pepper
2 ripe avocados

Finely chop the onion, pepper and radishes and stir into the yogurt with the walnuts, parsley and chives. Season to taste. Just before serving, cut the avocados in half lengthways and remove the stones. Pile the yogurt mixture on to the avocado halves and serve immediately.

Serves 4

Prawn appetiser

$\frac{1}{2}$ a cucumber, sliced
25 g (1 oz) butter
1 small onion, skinned and finely chopped
5 ml (1 level tsp) curry powder
100 g (4 oz) peeled prawns
150 ml ($\frac{1}{4}$ pint) natural yogurt
freshly ground sea salt and pepper
paprika to garnish

Arrange the cucumber slices on four individual dishes or scallop shells. Melt the butter in a saucepan and cook the onion for 5–10 minutes, until lightly browned. Stir in the curry powder and cook for 1 minute. Add the prawns and cook for a further 2 minutes. Leave the mixture to cool. Add the yogurt and season to taste. Divide the mixture between the dishes and serve chilled, garnished with a little paprika.

Serves 4

Blue cheese dip

100 g (4 oz) Danish blue or Roquefort cheese, softened
75 g (3 oz) curd cheese
15 ml (1 tbsp) lemon juice

Blend all the ingredients to a smooth cream and serve on tomato halves or with fingers of wholemeal bread. This could also be served as a party dip with spring onions, green pepper slices and carrot sticks.

Serves 4

Hummus

A traditional recipe from the Middle East

225 g (8 oz) chick peas, soaked (see page 23)
juice of 2 large lemons
150 ml ($\frac{1}{4}$ pint) tahini paste
60 ml (4 tbsp) olive oil
1–2 garlic cloves, skinned and crushed
freshly ground sea salt and pepper
chopped fresh parsley to garnish

Drain the peas, place in a saucepan and cover with cold water. Bring to the boil and simmer gently for 2 hours or until tender. Add more boiling water, if necessary, to keep the peas covered with water throughout the cooking time.

Drain the peas, reserving a little of the liquid. Put the peas in a blender, reserving a few for garnish, and gradually add the reserved liquid and the lemon juice, blending well after each addition to form a smooth purée. Add the tahini paste, oil and garlic and season to taste. Blend again until smooth. Spoon into a serving dish and sprinkle with the reserved chick peas and the chopped parsley. Serve with wholemeal bread.

Serves 8

Lemony bean appetiser

100 g (4 oz) flageolet beans, soaked (see page 23)
225 g (8 oz) firm tomatoes, skinned

For the dressing
finely grated rind and juice of 1 lemon
90 ml (6 tbsp) olive oil
1 garlic clove, skinned and crushed
15 ml (1 level tbsp) chopped fresh chives
freshly ground sea salt and pepper

Drain the flageolets and cook in boiling water for about 1 hour, until tender. Drain well.

Put the lemon rind and juice, the oil, garlic, chives and seasonings in a screw-topped jar and shake vigorously. Pour over the warm beans and leave to cool. Cover and chill.

Thinly slice the tomatoes and arrange on four individual serving plates or scallop shells. Pile the beans on to the tomatoes and serve with wholemeal bread.

Serves 4

Curried fenugreek and apple salad

50 g (2 oz) sprouted fenugreek
2 medium cooking apples, cored and finely chopped
50 g (2 oz) sultanas

For the dressing
5 ml (1 level tsp) curry powder
1 garlic clove, skinned and crushed
150 ml ($\frac{1}{4}$ pint) natural yogurt
freshly ground sea salt and pepper

Place the fenugreek in a bowl with the apples and sultanas. Mix the curry powder and garlic into the yogurt, season and fold the dressing into the salad. Divide the salad between four small bowls or plates and serve with wholemeal bread.

Serves 4

Alphotoco sprout and Double Gloucester salad

50 g (2 oz) sprouted alphotoco
225 g (8 oz) tomatoes, finely chopped
175 g (6 oz) Double Gloucester cheese, diced
60 ml (4 level tbsp) chopped fresh parsley to garnish

For the dressing
60 ml (4 tbsp) olive or sunflower oil
30 ml (2 tbsp) white wine vinegar
15 ml (1 level tbsp) tomato purée
5 ml (1 level tsp) paprika
a few drops of Tabasco sauce

Place the sprouts in a bowl and mix in the tomatoes and cheese. Whisk the oil, vinegar, tomato purée, paprika and Tabasco together and stir into the salad. Divide the salad between four small bowls and scatter the parsley over the top.

Serves 4

Avocado ramekins

1 large ripe avocado
grated rind and juice of 1 lemon
100 g (4 oz) curd cheese
1 small garlic clove, skinned and crushed
freshly ground sea salt and pepper
60 ml (4 tbsp) natural yogurt
sprigs of parsley to garnish

Stone and peel the avocado and mash the flesh with a fork. Blend with all the remaining ingredients, except the parsley, until smooth. Spoon into four ramekin dishes and leave in the refrigerator to chill for about 30 minutes. Garnish each dish with a sprig of parsley and serve immediately with fingers of wholemeal toast.

Serves 4

Red cherry soup

450 g (1 lb) red cherries, washed
150 ml ($\frac{1}{4}$ pint) water
1 cinnamon stick
pared rind of $\frac{1}{2}$ a lemon
15 ml (1 level tbsp) Barbados sugar
150 ml ($\frac{1}{4}$ pint) red wine
150 ml ($\frac{1}{4}$ pint) natural yogurt

Stone the cherries, reserving the stones, and gently simmer the cherries in a saucepan with the water, cinnamon, lemon rind and sugar for about 10 minutes until soft. Boil the cherry stones with the wine for a few minutes and strain. Remove the cinnamon stick and lemon rind and pour the strained wine into the cherry pulp. Purée the mixture in a blender or rub through a sieve. Stir the yogurt into the cherry pulp and chill in the refrigerator before serving.

Serves 4

Cream of watercress soup

1 bunch of watercress, trimmed and washed
7 g ($\frac{1}{4}$ oz) butter
300 ml ($\frac{1}{2}$ pint) chicken stock
freshly ground sea salt and pepper
150 ml ($\frac{1}{4}$ pint) buttermilk

Reserve a few watercress sprigs. Chop the remainder and cook lightly in the butter for 2–3 minutes. Add the stock and seasoning and simmer for 15–20 minutes. Sieve and return to the heat. Add the buttermilk and heat gently without boiling. Serve garnished with the reserved sprigs of watercress.

Serves 2

Aubergine starter

450 g (1 lb) aubergines
25 g (1 oz) butter
1 garlic clove, skinned and finely chopped
1 medium onion, skinned and chopped
1 slice of wholemeal bread, cubed
15 ml (1 tbsp) lemon juice
30 ml (2 level tbsp) chopped fresh parsley
freshly ground sea salt and pepper
30 ml (2 tbsp) sunflower oil
fresh parsley sprigs to garnish

Pierce the aubergines with a fork and place them on a baking sheet. Bake in the oven at 190°C (375°F) mark 5 for 45 minutes until soft. Allow to cool slightly, then cut the aubergines in half and scoop out the flesh.

Meanwhile, melt the butter in a saucepan and fry the garlic and onion for 5 minutes until soft. Purée the aubergine flesh, the garlic, onion, bread, lemon juice, parsley and seasoning in a blender until smooth. Gradually add the oil, blending well after each addition. Spoon into individual ramekin dishes and chill in the refrigerator for 1 hour. Garnish with sprigs of parsley and serve with lightly buttered wholemeal toast.

Serves 6

Mushroom and tomato starter

175 g (6 oz) tomatoes, skinned and thinly sliced
225 g (8 oz) mushrooms, wiped and sliced
75 g (3 oz) lean unsmoked bacon
4 slices of granary bread, toasted
chopped fresh parsley to garnish

For the dressing
60 ml (4 tbsp) sunflower oil
15 ml (1 level tbsp) tomato purée
15 ml (1 tbsp) white wine vinegar
1.25 ml ($\frac{1}{4}$ tsp) Worcestershire sauce
pinch of mustard powder
freshly ground sea salt and pepper

Arrange the tomatoes and mushrooms in layers in a shallow bowl. Whisk all the dressing ingredients together until well blended, then pour over the tomatoes and mushrooms. Cover and leave overnight in the refrigerator.

Just before serving, grill the bacon until crisp and golden brown and snip into small pieces. Pile the mushroom and tomato mixture equally on to the slices of toasted granary bread, draining off any excess marinade. Sprinkle with pieces of bacon and garnish with parsley, then serve immediately.

Serves 4

Egg flower soup

1.1 litres (2 pints) chicken stock
6 eggs
30 ml (2 tbsp) tamari sauce
5 ml (1 tsp) white wine vinegar
2 spring onions, finely chopped, to garnish

Heat the stock in a saucepan. Meanwhile, beat the eggs well, then pour into the stock in a thin stream, stirring all the time. Add the tamari sauce and vinegar and simmer for 1 minute. Garnish with chopped spring onions.

Serves 4

Gazpacho

450 g (1 lb) tomatoes, skinned and sliced
1 small onion, skinned and finely chopped
1 small green pepper, seeded and finely chopped
1 garlic clove, skinned and crushed
15 ml (1 tbsp) white wine vinegar
15 ml (1 tbsp) olive oil
15 ml (1 tbsp) lemon juice
freshly ground sea salt and pepper
$\frac{1}{4}$ of a cucumber, diced
wholemeal bread croûtons (see page 76)

Combine the tomatoes, onion, green pepper, garlic, vinegar and olive oil in a blender. Turn into a bowl, add the lemon juice and season to taste. Cover and chill thoroughly in the refrigerator. Serve sprinkled with the diced cucumber and croûtons.

Serves 4

Pear and grape salad

1 lettuce, washed
2 pears, peeled, halved and cored
100 g (4 oz) curd cheese or cottage cheese, sieved
freshly ground sea salt and pepper
5 ml (1 level tsp) chopped fresh chives
30 ml (2 tbsp) French dressing (see page 172)
50 g (2 oz) black grapes, halved and pipped

Arrange the lettuce on a serving plate and put the pear halves on top. Blend the cheese, seasoning and chives together, adding a very little milk, if necessary, to soften the mixture. Spoon the cheese mixture into the pear hollows and chill well. Sprinkle with French dressing before serving and garnish with the grape halves.

Serves 4

Sausage, apple and pasta soup

225 g (8 oz) sausages
1 small green pepper, seeded and finely diced
1 large onion, skinned and grated
1 large eating apple, peeled, cored and grated
450 g (1 lb) tomatoes, skinned and quartered
900 ml (1½ pints) vegetable stock
150 ml (¼ pint) dry cider
50 g (2 oz) wholewheat short cut macaroni
freshly ground sea salt and pepper
50 g (2 oz) Double Gloucester cheese, grated

Grill the sausages for 15–20 minutes, turning occasionally, until golden brown. Cut each into four pieces. Put the sausages and all the remaining ingredients, except the grated cheese, into a large saucepan and cook for 30–40 minutes until the vegetables and pasta are tender. Spoon into four warmed serving bowls and sprinkle with grated cheese. Serve with warm wholemeal rolls.

Serves 4

Red bean and bacon soup

100 g (4 oz) red kidney beans, soaked (see page 23)
10 ml (2 tsp) sunflower oil
1 large onion, skinned and finely chopped
225-g (8-oz) lean bacon joint, cubed
1 small red pepper, seeded and finely diced
450 g (1 lb) tomatoes, skinned and quartered
1.1 litres (2 pints) chicken stock
freshly ground sea salt and pepper
15 ml (1 level tbsp) tomato purée
a few drops of Tabasco sauce
10 ml (2 level tsp) paprika

Drain and rinse the kidney beans, then drain again. Heat the oil in a large saucepan and sauté the onion, bacon and pepper for 2–3 minutes until just soft. Add the remaining ingredients and bring to the boil. Cover and simmer for 1¼–1½ hours or until the beans are tender. Serve with fresh granary bread or rolls.

Serves 4

Montego pepperpot

This is a smooth, creamy soup with a subtle flavour of coconut. There are many variations in the West Indies, some rather more solid and meaty than this very tasty Jamaican version.

1 medium onion, skinned and finely chopped
225 g (8 oz) spinach, trimmed, washed and chopped
$\frac{1}{4}$ of a medium white cabbage, shredded
225 g (8 oz) prawns or shrimps
600 ml (1 pint) beef or chicken stock
freshly ground sea salt
4 ml ($\frac{3}{4}$ level tsp) cayenne pepper
50 g (2 oz) block creamed coconut
150 ml ($\frac{1}{4}$ pint) hot water

Put the onion, spinach and cabbage into a saucepan and add the prawns or shrimps, reserving a few for garnish. (The shells can be left on to give extra flavour.) Add the stock and seasonings, bring to the boil, cover and simmer for 30 minutes, until the vegetables are tender.

Strain the mixture into another pan. Dissolve the creamed coconut in the hot water, add to the pan and bring slowly to the boil. Serve very hot, garnished with the remaining prawns and accompanied by toasted wholemeal croûtons (see page 76) or wholemeal crispbread.

Serves 4

Lentil and carrot soup

225 g (8 oz) red lentils
1.1 litres (2 pints) chicken stock
350 g (12 oz) carrots, trimmed and scrubbed
25 g (1 oz) vegetable margarine
1 medium onion, skinned and finely chopped
1 garlic clove, skinned and crushed
4 sticks of celery, trimmed, washed and sliced
2 medium potatoes, peeled and diced
freshly ground sea salt and pepper

Rinse the lentils and place in a large saucepan with the stock. Bring to the boil, then simmer for 10 minutes, removing any scum that forms with a slotted spoon. Dice 225 g (8 oz) carrots, reserving the remainder.

Melt the margarine in a saucepan and sauté the onion, garlic, celery, diced carrot and potato for 5 minutes. Add to the stock and lentils and season well. Simmer for about 1 hour, until the vegetables are tender.

Cut the remaining carrots into thin strips and cook in boiling salted water for about 3 minutes. Drain and sprinkle over the top of the soup. Serve with wholemeal bread.

Serves 4

Chunky courgette soup

Illustrated in colour opposite

100 g (4 oz) haricot beans, soaked (see page 23)
350 g (12 oz) potatoes
225 g (8 oz) courgettes, trimmed
350 g (12 oz) leeks, trimmed and washed
1 garlic clove, skinned and crushed
30 ml (2 tbsp) sunflower oil
50 g (2 oz) butter or vegetable margarine
1.1 litres (2 pints) chicken stock
freshly ground sea salt and pepper
5 ml (1 level tsp) chopped fresh basil
100 g (4 oz) Cheddar cheese, grated
chopped fresh parsley to garnish

Drain the beans and place in a saucepan. Cover with fresh water and simmer, covered, for 1½ hours, until tender, then drain well.

Peel and dice the potatoes and cut the courgettes into chunky slices about 0.5 cm (¼ inch) thick. Chop the leeks finely. Combine the garlic with the leeks.

Heat the oil in a frying pan and fry the potato for 2–3 minutes. Drain, using a slotted spoon, and place in a large saucepan. Lightly fry the leeks for about 5 minutes, stirring frequently, drain and add to the potato. Lastly, melt the butter or vegetable margarine, add the courgettes and cook for about 5 minutes. Add to the pan with the beans.

Pour over the stock, season and add the basil. Simmer, covered, for 1¼ hours, until the vegetables are tender. Sprinkle the cheese over the soup during the last 15 minutes of cooking. Check the seasoning just before serving garnished with chopped parsley.

Serves 6–8

Leek and potato soup

25 g (1 oz) vegetable margarine
900 g (2 lb) leeks, trimmed, sliced and washed
1 medium onion, skinned and chopped
450 g (1 lb) potatoes, peeled and sliced
1.1 litres (2 pints) vegetable stock
freshly ground sea salt and pepper
chopped fresh chives to garnish

Melt the margarine in a large saucepan and sauté the vegetables for 5 minutes. Add the stock and seasoning and bring to the boil. Cover and simmer for about 45 minutes, until the vegetables are tender.

Cool the soup, then purée in a blender or rub through a sieve. Return to a clean pan and reheat. If too thick, add a little more stock or some milk and adjust the seasoning. Sprinkle with chopped chives and serve with granary bread.

Serves 4

Grapefruit, alfalfa and cheese salad

Illustrated in colour opposite

2 large grapefruit
175 g (6 oz) curd cheese or home-made
cream cheese (see page 207)
50 g (2 oz) sunflower seeds
50 g (2 oz) sprouted alfalfa to garnish

Cut the rind and pith from the grapefruit. Cut each grapefruit in half lengthways and
then cut each half into six crossways slices. Arrange these in four small dishes and put a
portion of cheese on the top. Scatter the sunflower seeds over the cheese and garnish
with sprouted alfalfa.

Serves 4

Liptauer cheese

Illustrated in colour opposite

350 g (12 oz) cottage cheese
175 g (6 oz) Cheddar cheese, grated
100 g (4 oz) butter, softened
45 ml (3 level tbsp) chopped fresh chives
15 ml (1 tbsp) cider vinegar
30 ml (2 level tbsp) finely chopped onion
10 ml (2 level tsp) French mustard
10 ml (2 level tsp) paprika
5 ml (1 level tsp) caraway seeds
2 anchovy fillets, finely chopped

Combine the cheeses and butter in a bowl by creaming together until smooth. Work in
the remaining ingredients. Serve with wholemeal toast. This cheese can be made in
advance and kept, covered, in the refrigerator for up to two weeks.

Serves 4

Apricot, cheese and ham salad

100 g (4 oz) lean ham, chopped
100 g (4 oz) curd cheese
1 small cucumber, thinly sliced
4 apricots, stoned and quartered

Mix the ham into the cheese. Arrange a circle of cucumber slices round the edge of four
small plates and put the ham and cheese mixture in the middle. Prop the apricot pieces
upright against the piles of cheese so the finished dishes resemble waterlilies.

Serves 4

Bortsch

2 medium onions, skinned and finely chopped
2 large carrots, trimmed, scrubbed and finely chopped
700 g (1½ lb) raw beetroot, skinned and grated
225 g (8 oz) cabbage, trimmed, shredded and washed
2 sprigs of fresh parsley
1 bay leaf
freshly ground sea salt and pepper
2.3 litres (4 pints) chicken stock
juice of 1 lemon
150 ml (¼ pint) soured cream or natural yogurt

Put the prepared vegetables, the parsley, bay leaf, seasoning and chicken stock into a saucepan, bring to the boil and simmer for 30 minutes or until the vegetables are tender. Remove the bay leaf and rub the soup through a sieve or purée in a blender until smooth. Add the lemon juice. Serve the soup in individual bowls with a spoonful of soured cream or yogurt on top of each.

Serves 6–8

Butter bean and tomato soup

175 g (6 oz) butter beans, soaked (see page 23)
15 ml (1 tbsp) sunflower oil
1 large onion, skinned and chopped
100 g (4 oz) lean unsmoked bacon, rinded and chopped
1.1 litres (2 pints) chicken stock
450 g (1 lb) tomatoes, skinned and quartered
30 ml (2 level tbsp) tomato purée
1 bay leaf
freshly ground sea salt and pepper

Drain and rinse the beans, then drain again. Heat the oil in a large saucepan and fry the onion and bacon for 5 minutes until soft. Add the beans and the remaining ingredients, season to taste and bring to the boil. Cover and simmer for 2 hours, or until the butter beans are tender. Serve hot with fresh wholemeal bread.

Serves 4

Golden haddock mousses

350 g (12 oz) smoked haddock fillet
175 g (6 oz) curd cheese
600 ml (1 pint) natural yogurt
grated rind and juice of $\frac{1}{2}$ a lemon
freshly ground sea salt and pepper
15 g ($\frac{1}{2}$ oz) powdered gelatine
lemon slices and parsley sprigs to garnish

Poach the fish in a little water in a frying pan for about 10 minutes, until tender. Remove the skin and bones and flake the fish into a bowl. Blend the cheese, yogurt, lemon rind and juice and seasoning together and add to the fish.

Put 45 ml (3 tbsp) water in a small bowl over a pan of hot water, sprinkle over the gelatine and heat until dissolved. Cool, then stir into the fish mixture. Spoon into eight individual ramekin dishes and leave in the refrigerator to set. Garnish with lemon slices and a sprig of parsley and serve with fingers of wholemeal toast.

Serves 8

Cheese and nut slices

100 g (4 oz) walnuts or hazelnuts, finely ground
100 g (4 oz) curd cheese
2.5 ml ($\frac{1}{2}$ level tsp) paprika
30 ml (2 level tbsp) chopped fresh chives
freshly ground sea salt and pepper
a little milk, if required

Blend all the ingredients together, adding a little milk if the mixture is too stiff, and season well. Form into a roll and leave in a cool place or in the refrigerator for about 30 minutes. Serve in slices with a tomato salad.

Serves 4

Garlic cheese

100 g (4 oz) curd cheese or cottage cheese, sieved
1 garlic clove, skinned and crushed
15 ml (1 tbsp) natural yogurt
freshly ground sea salt and pepper
cucumber and tomato slices
chopped fresh parsley to garnish

Blend the cheese, garlic and yogurt to a soft cream and season to taste. Arrange the cucumber and tomato slices on four individual serving plates and spoon the mixture on top. Sprinkle with chopped parsley.

Serves 4

Cheese and pepper starter

100 g (4 oz) curd cheese or cottage cheese, sieved
15 ml (1 tbsp) natural yogurt
$\frac{1}{2}$ a green pepper, seeded and finely chopped
$\frac{1}{2}$ a red pepper, seeded and finely chopped
freshly ground sea salt and pepper
1 lettuce, washed

Blend the curd cheese and yogurt to a soft cream. Stir in the green and red peppers and season to taste. Serve on lettuce leaves with wholemeal biscuits or crispbread.

Serves 4

Chicken and watercress soup

225 g (8 oz) cold cooked chicken, diced
15 ml (1 tbsp) tamari sauce
5 ml (1 tsp) sunflower oil
1.1 litres (2 pints) chicken stock
2 bunches of watercress, trimmed, washed and chopped

Put the chicken into a bowl and mix well with the tamari sauce and oil, then leave for about 30 minutes.

Bring the stock to the boil in a large saucepan, add the watercress, stir well and, when the soup comes to the boil again, add the meat mixture. Simmer for 15 minutes or until the watercress is tender and serve hot.

Serves 4

Cucumber portugaise

2 large cucumbers
1 medium onion, skinned and finely chopped
60 ml (4 tbsp) sunflower oil
4 firm medium tomatoes, skinned, seeded and chopped
10 ml (2 level tsp) tomato purée
30 ml (2 tbsp) garlic vinegar
2.5 ml ($\frac{1}{2}$ level tsp) chopped fresh thyme
freshly ground sea salt and pepper

Thinly pare the cucumbers using a potato peeler, then cut them into 2.5-cm (1-inch) lengths. Cut each piece into quarters, lengthways, and remove the centre seeds with the point of a knife. Plunge the pieces into boiling salted water for 5 minutes. Drain, refresh under cold running water and drain again.

Sauté the onion in the oil for 3–4 minutes or until soft, then add the tomatoes, the tomato purée, vinegar and thyme. Blend the cucumber pieces with the tomato mixture and season well. Chill and serve with crusty wholemeal bread.

Serves 4

Stuffed eggs

4 eggs
50 g (2 oz) Cheddar cheese, grated
2.5 ml ($\frac{1}{2}$ level tsp) mustard powder
freshly ground sea salt and pepper
30 ml (2 tbsp) mayonnaise (see page 171)
1 bunch of watercress, trimmed and washed
capers and radishes to garnish

Cook the eggs in boiling water for 10 minutes. Cool under cold running water and shell. Cut each egg in half, lengthways, and scoop out the yolks. Set aside the whites.

Mix the yolks with the cheese, mustard, salt and pepper and moisten with the mayonnaise. Pile the mixture back into the whites. Arrange the stuffed eggs on a bed of watercress and garnish with capers and radishes.

Serves 4

Cucumber dip

150 g (5 oz) cucumber
freshly ground sea salt
1 garlic clove, skinned
5 ml (1 level tsp) chopped fresh parsley
150 ml ($\frac{1}{4}$ pint) natural yogurt
5 ml (1 tsp) clear honey

Very finely dice the cucumber. Sprinkle lightly with salt and leave to stand for about 30 minutes, then drain well. Rub the garlic clove round the inside of a small serving bowl. Stir the parsley into the yogurt and add the honey. Stir in the cucumber and spoon the dip into the prepared serving bowl. Serve chilled, with fingers of wholemeal toast.

Serves 4

Guacamole

2 avocados
2 medium tomatoes, skinned
1 small onion, skinned and chopped
15 ml (1 level tbsp) chopped fresh parsley
1 green pepper, seeded and chopped
freshly ground sea salt and pepper

Peel, stone and mash the avocado flesh. Halve the tomatoes and discard the seeds. Chop the flesh and add with the onion, parsley and green pepper to the avocado pulp. Adjust the seasoning and serve in small bowls as a starter with fingers of wholemeal toast.

Serves 4

NOTE Guacamole should not be prepared too far in advance as the avocado will discolour.

Split pea soup

225 g (8 oz) green split peas, washed
1.1 litres (2 pints) ham stock
100-g (4-oz) piece of lean unsmoked bacon
1 medium carrot, trimmed, scrubbed and sliced
2 sticks of celery, trimmed, washed and sliced
1 medium onion, skinned and chopped
bouquet garni
freshly ground sea salt and pepper
chopped fresh parsley to garnish

Place all the ingredients, except the chopped parsley, in a large saucepan, bring to the boil, then simmer for about 1 hour until the peas and vegetables are soft. Remove the bacon from the soup and chop into small pieces. Remove the bouquet garni, then rub the soup through a sieve or purée in a blender until smooth. Return to the saucepan, add the bacon pieces and reheat to serve. Sprinkle with parsley and serve with chunks of granary bread.

Serves 4

Avocado and orange salad platter

3 large oranges, peeled and segmented
1 avocado
12 black olives
1 small onion, skinned and sliced
chopped fresh parsley to garnish

For the dressing
60 ml (4 tbsp) olive oil
freshly ground sea salt and pepper
a dash of Tabasco sauce
30 ml (2 tbsp) lemon juice

Make the dressing by whisking the ingredients together until well blended, or put them in a screw-topped jar and shake vigorously.

Arrange the orange segments in the bottom of a serving dish. Stone and peel the avocado and slice into fingers, add the dressing and toss lightly. Spoon the avocado mixture on to the oranges and arrange the olives and onion rings on top. Serve at once, sprinkled with chopped parsley.

Serves 4

Egg and yogurt mayonnaise

1 lettuce, washed
$\frac{1}{2}$ a cucumber, sliced
4 hard-boiled eggs, sliced
150 ml ($\frac{1}{4}$ pint) natural yogurt
5 ml (1 tsp) lemon juice
1 stick of celery, trimmed, washed and chopped
4 pimiento-stuffed olives, chopped
15 ml (1 level tbsp) chopped fresh chives
freshly ground sea salt and pepper
watercress and parsley sprigs or paprika to garnish

Arrange the lettuce leaves and most of the cucumber slices on a large oval plate. Chop the remaining cucumber and use in the dressing. Overlap slices of hard-boiled egg down the centre of the lettuce leaves. Beat together the yogurt, lemon juice, celery, olives, cucumber and chives. Season to taste and spoon over the eggs before serving. Garnish with sprigs of watercress and parsley or sprinkle with paprika.

Serves 4

Tomato, watercress and cheese salad

350 g (12 oz) tomatoes
1 bunch of watercress
50 g (2 oz) currants
100 g (4 oz) curd cheese or home-made
cream cheese (see page 207)

For the dressing
60 ml (4 tbsp) olive or sunflower oil
30 ml (2 tbsp) white wine vinegar
15 ml (1 level tbsp) tomato purée
a few drops of Tabasco sauce
1 garlic clove, skinned and crushed
freshly ground sea salt and pepper

Finely chop the tomatoes and watercress and divide them, with the currants, between four small bowls. To make the dressing, whisk the oil, vinegar, tomato purée, Tabasco, garlic and seasoning together until well blended and pour over the salads. Put a portion of cheese on top of each.

Serves 4

Everyday Family Fare

No matter how much enthusiasm you may have for wholefoods, introducing them to your family might prove a little difficult. It may be some time before they will give up such bad habits as munching sweets, helping themselves to biscuits and frying up hamburgers to put into white bread rolls. What is your plan of campaign?

If you start by laying down the law, banning junk foods from the house and emphasising continually that 'wholefood is *good* for you', you aren't going to get anywhere. You will probably end up with a rebellion on your hands and the dinner table will become your battleground.

You have got to go about things in a more subtle way. Anyone who eats wholefoods regularly will agree that they taste better, so start off by gradually introducing them into the house and offering them as an alternative to the foods that perhaps your family regards now as more 'normal'. Put a delicious, nutty wholemeal loaf on to the bread board with the white, muesli beside the cereals at breakfast, and offer an imaginative salad as well as cooked vegetables with the main meal. Then gradually replace the processed foods in your larder with basic wholefood ingredients and you will find that the new eating habits have evolved naturally.

Sweets can be a great problem with children. If you are starting out with a new baby it will obviously be easy for you. If he is not given sweets from the start, he will not expect them later on. Bring him up on yogurt and fresh fruits and later on, instead of sweets, give him dried fruits and nuts and the occasional muesli bar. Any attempt at banning sweets and soft drinks from older children who are used to them could lead to their deceiving you, so a compromise is the best thing. Have fruits, nuts and natural fruit juices in the house, but leave them to make their own decisions as to what they do outside. At least you will have given them a healthy alternative, and in the end they will probably realise that they like your ideas as much as, if not better than, their own.

It may not be only the family's taste that has to adapt when you change to wholefoods. You might well have to adapt your cooking, too. Gradually, you will leave the chip pan in the cupboard and the frying pan will be brought out less frequently. All your cooking methods will be light and might well require less fat; and you may have to learn new techniques with wholemeal flour and other new ingredients such as brown rice. It will help at first to follow recipes, such as the ones in this book, which use all the possible ingredients in a variety of ways. When you are used to them and want to try something new, you will not have to replace all your cookery books with new ones since most recipes can be adapted to wholefood ingredients and methods.

Once your family have learned to know and enjoy what's good for them, varying the family's main meals every day need be no problem. The wholefood cook has so many basic ingredients from which to choose, and the dishes that can be made with them are so numerous that the structure of the meal need never be the same from day to day. Meat or fish with the traditional accompaniment of two vegetables or a salad can still be served and, still keeping to the same pattern, you can change the meat dish to a vegetarian savoury such as a cheese or egg dish, a bean casserole or nut croquettes. Instead of potatoes, try one of the other accompanying dishes such as pasta or rice.

These accompaniments can also form the basis of very substantial meals, such as lasagne, which need no accompaniment other than a lightly cooked vegetable or a salad. Home-made pizzas are very satisfying to make and provide a simple meal with the 'filler' part and the protein all in one. They too need only a salad accompaniment.

Salads can be main courses as well as side dishes. You can mix the protein (beans, diced meat, flaked fish) part with the vegetables or into its own separate salad dressing so you can have a vegetable salad on the side rather than a mixture. You can serve baked jacket potatoes with a main course salad or a cold dish of rice or bulgar wheat.

After a while, wholefood cooking and eating will become a natural part of life and the whole family will be fully satisfied right through the week.

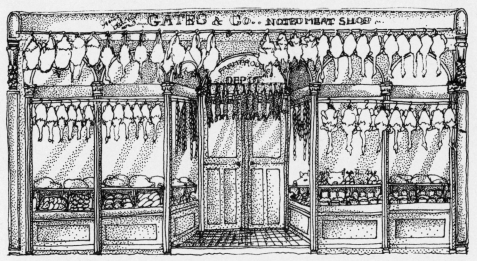

Somerset chicken

4 chicken portions, skinned
15 ml (1 level tbsp) mustard powder
freshly ground sea salt and pepper
300 ml ($\frac{1}{2}$ pint) cider
30 ml (2 tbsp) clear honey

Place the chicken in a large shallow dish. Mix the remaining ingredients, except the parsley, together and pour over the chicken. Leave to marinate for at least 1 hour.

Put the chicken portions and marinade into the grill pan and grill under a medium heat for 20 minutes. Turn the portions over and grill for a further 20–30 minutes, basting with the marinade from time to time, until tender and golden. Place the chicken in a heated serving dish and pour over any remaining marinade.

Serves 4

Casserole of kidney, tomato and bacon

6 lambs' kidneys, skinned and cored
4 rashers of lean unsmoked bacon
4 large tomatoes, sliced
freshly ground sea salt and pepper

Cut the kidneys into even-sized pieces. Rind the bacon and fry the rinds to extract the fat, then fry the kidneys lightly for about 5 minutes until lightly browned. (It may be necessary to add a little vegetable fat or oil.)

Put the kidney pieces into an ovenproof casserole and arrange the tomato slices on top. Season and add the bacon. Cover and cook in the oven at 180°C (350°F) mark 4 for 30 minutes or until the meat is tender.

Serves 4

Butter bean and tuna gratin

400 ml ($\frac{3}{4}$ pint) milk
small piece of onion
small piece of carrot
1 bay leaf
6 peppercorns
blade of fresh mace
225 g (8 oz) butter beans, soaked (see page 23)
450 g (1 lb) broccoli, trimmed
198-g (7-oz) can tuna fish, drained
freshly ground sea salt and pepper
40 g ($1\frac{1}{2}$ oz) butter
60 ml (4 level tbsp) plain wholemeal flour
freshly grated Parmesan cheese

Pour the milk into a pan and add the onion, carrot, bay leaf, peppercorns and mace. Bring slowly to the boil. Remove from the heat and leave, covered, to infuse until cold.

Drain the butter beans and cook gently in boiling water for about $1\frac{1}{2}$ hours until tender. Drain well.

Meanwhile, break the broccoli into florets and cook in a little boiling salted water for about 10 minutes until just tender. Drain and arrange in a buttered, shallow, oval ovenproof dish. Flake the tuna with a fork, combine with the cooked beans and season with salt and pepper. Pile this mixture down the centre of the dish.

Strain the infused milk. Melt the butter in a saucepan, stir in the flour and cook for 1–2 minutes. Remove the pan from the heat, gradually add the milk and season. Return to the heat and stir continuously until the sauce boils and thickens. Lower the heat and simmer for a further 2–3 minutes. Pour this sauce over the tuna and broccoli. Sprinkle well with grated Parmesan and bake in the oven at 200°C (400°F) mark 6 for 15–20 minutes until golden and bubbling.

Serves 4

Baked stuffed plaice

1 medium plaice, cleaned and head removed
75 g (3 oz) Cheddar cheese, finely cubed
2 tomatoes, skinned and chopped
25 g (1 oz) brown rice, cooked
freshly ground sea salt and pepper
25 g (1 oz) butter, melted
40 g (1½ oz) Cheddar cheese, grated
50 g (2 oz) fresh wholemeal breadcrumbs
chopped fresh parsley and lemon slices to garnish

Wash the fish thoroughly and, using a sharp knife, make an incision in the white skin along the backbone. Loosen the flesh from the bone on each side as far as the fins but not right through the skin. Mix together the cheese cubes, chopped tomatoes and rice, season and use to fill the cavity in the fish.

Place the fish on a greased baking sheet and brush with melted butter. Mix together the grated cheese and breadcrumbs and sprinkle over the fish. Bake in the oven at 200°C (400°F) mark 6 for 20–25 minutes, or until the fish is cooked and slightly flaky. Serve garnished with parsley and lemon slices.

Serves 2

Vegetable spice lasagne

1 aubergine, trimmed
175 g (6 oz) wholewheat lasagne
15 g (½ oz) vegetable margarine
1 large onion, skinned and thinly sliced
3 large courgettes, trimmed, washed and thinly sliced
4 large tomatoes, skinned and thinly sliced
freshly ground sea salt and pepper
1.25 ml (¼ level tsp) ground nutmeg
1.25 ml (¼ level tsp) ground mace
225 g (8 oz) Bel Paese cheese, thinly sliced
300 ml (½ pint) natural yogurt

Slice the aubergine thinly and sprinkle with salt. Leave for 30 minutes to drain off excess juice, then rinse off the salt. Cook the lasagne in boiling salted water for 15 minutes, drain well and rinse under cold water.

Melt the margarine in a large saucepan. Add the aubergine, onion and courgettes and sauté for 15 minutes until soft. Add the tomatoes, seasoning and spices and cook for a further 2 minutes.

Layer the vegetables, lasagne and 175 g (6 oz) cheese in a greased 1.7-litre (3-pint) shallow ovenproof dish. Pour the yogurt over and top with the remaining cheese slices.

Bake in the oven at 190°C (375°F) mark 5 for 45 minutes, until the top is golden.

Serves 4

Moussaka

30 ml (2 tbsp) sunflower or olive oil
1 large onion, skinned and sliced
1 garlic clove, skinned and crushed
450 g (1 lb) lean minced lamb
350 g (12 oz) potatoes, peeled and thinly sliced
2 aubergines, washed and thinly sliced
450 g (1 lb) tomatoes, skinned and sliced
freshly ground sea salt and pepper

For the cheese sauce
25 g (1 oz) butter
25 g (1 oz) plain wholemeal flour
300 ml ($\frac{1}{2}$ pint) milk
50 g (2 oz) Cheddar or Parmesan cheese, grated
freshly ground sea salt and pepper

For the yogurt topping
1 egg, beaten
25 g (1 oz) plain wholemeal flour
150 ml ($\frac{1}{4}$ pint) natural yogurt
freshly ground sea salt and pepper

Heat the oil in a frying pan. Add the onion and garlic and cook for 3–4 minutes, until soft. Stir in the lamb and cook quickly for about 5 minutes, until brown. Remove from the heat.

Make the cheese sauce by melting the butter in a saucepan. Add the flour and cook for 1–2 minutes. Remove from the heat and gradually stir in the milk. Return to the heat and cook, stirring, until the sauce is boiling and thickened. Simmer for 2–3 minutes, then stir in the cheese and continue cooking until it melts. Season with salt and pepper.

Arrange half the potato slices in the bottom of a deep 2.3-litre (4-pint) ovenproof dish. Add layers of the other vegetables, the meat and the cheese sauce, seasoning each layer. Finish with a layer of potato slices. Bake in the oven at 190°C (375°F) mark 5 for 35 minutes.

For the topping, blend the egg and flour together, then stir in the yogurt and season well. Spoon on top of the potato slices and return the casserole to the oven for a further 25 minutes, or until the topping is set and browned.

Serves 6

Tomato pizza

6 large tomatoes, skinned and chopped
2 medium onions, skinned and chopped
30 ml (2 level tbsp) tomato purée
freshly ground sea salt and pepper
225 g (8 oz) wholemeal pizza dough (see page 111)
5 ml (1 level tsp) chopped fresh marjoram
4 anchovy fillets
6 black olives, stoned and chopped
175–225 g (6–8 oz) Bel Paese or Mozzarella cheese, sliced
chopped fresh parsley to garnish

Mix together the tomatoes, onions and tomato purée and season with salt and pepper.
Roll out the pizza dough on a lightly floured surface to form a 23-cm (9-inch) round.
Spread the tomato mixture on top and sprinkle with marjoram. Arrange the anchovy
fillets and olives over the mixture and top with the cheese slices. Bake in the oven at
220°C (425°F) mark 7 for 20 minutes or until the cheese is melted and golden brown.
Serve hot, sprinkled with a little chopped parsley.

Serves 4

Vegetable pot

40 g (1½ oz) vegetable margarine
1 onion, skinned and sliced
3 courgettes, trimmed, washed and sliced
1 small green pepper, seeded and sliced
1 garlic clove, skinned and crushed
2.5 ml (½ level tsp) ground coriander
2.5 ml (½ level tsp) ground cumin
40 g (1½ oz) plain wholemeal flour
600 ml (1 pint) vegetable stock
freshly ground sea salt and pepper
4 tomatoes, skinned
175 g (6 oz) haricot beans, soaked and
cooked (see page 23)
30 ml (2 level tbsp) tomato purée
15 ml (1 level tbsp) wheatgerm

Melt the margarine in a large saucepan and add the vegetables and spices. Sauté for
about 15 minutes until the vegetables are soft. Stir in the flour and cook for 2 minutes.
Gradually stir in the stock and bring to the boil to thicken, then season well.
    Roughly chop the tomatoes and stir into the pan with the beans and tomato purée.
Cover and simmer gently for 35 minutes, until all the vegetables are tender. Spoon into
a warm serving dish and sprinkle with the wheatgerm.

Serves 4

Chinese omelette

15 ml (1 tbsp) sunflower or groundnut oil
2 medium onions, skinned and chopped
1 garlic clove, skinned and crushed
4-cm (1½-inch) piece of root ginger, peeled and chopped
25 g (1 oz) brown rice
30 ml (2 tbsp) dry cider
10 ml (2 tsp) tamari sauce
300 ml (½ pint) chicken stock or water
freshly ground sea salt and pepper
4 bamboo shoots or sticks of celery, trimmed, washed and chopped
100 g (4 oz) mushrooms, wiped and chopped
100 g (4 oz) peeled shrimps
4 eggs
25 g (1 oz) butter

Heat the oil in a large frying pan. Add the onions, garlic and ginger and stir-fry (see page 150) for 3–4 minutes, until soft. Stir in the rice and stir-fry for 2 minutes. Add the cider, tamari sauce and stock, season with salt and bring to the boil. Reduce the heat and simmer for 25 minutes, stirring occasionally.

Stir in the bamboo shoots or celery and mushrooms and simmer for a further 10–15 minutes, until tender. Stir in the shrimps and continue cooking until heated through.

Beat the eggs, add 60 ml (4 tbsp) water and season with salt and pepper. Melt half the butter in a frying pan over a medium heat, tilting the pan so that the surface is evenly greased. Pour in half the egg mixture and gently stir with a fork, allowing the uncooked egg to flow to the sides to cook. Once the egg has set, stop stirring and cook the omelette for another minute until the under-side is golden brown. When the omelette is cooked, pile half the shrimp and rice mixture in the centre and fold up two sides of the omelette over the mixture. Turn the omelette on to a heated serving plate and keep warm while making a second omelette with the remaining butter, egg and shrimp mixture. Any remaining filling may be used as a garnish.

Serves 2

Grilled pork chops with apple rings

2 loin pork chops, trimmed of fat
15 ml (1 tbsp) olive oil
1 cooking apple, peeled, cored and sliced into rings

Brush the chops with olive oil. Place the apple rings in the base of the grill pan and put the chops on the grid. Grill the chops under a medium heat for 10–12 minutes on each side or until they are well cooked. When they are done, arrange them on a heated serving dish and keep hot. Put the apple rings on the grid and brown very lightly. Arrange on the serving dish with the chops.

Serves 2

Cheese flan

175 g (6 oz) wholemeal pastry (see page 237)
15 ml (1 tbsp) sunflower oil
1 medium onion, skinned and chopped
2 eggs
175 ml (6 fl oz) milk
freshly ground sea salt and pepper
2.5 ml ($\frac{1}{2}$ level tsp) prepared mustard
100 g (4 oz) Red Leicester cheese, grated

Line a 20.5-cm (8-inch) diameter flan ring with the pastry. Prick the base with a fork.
Heat the oil and fry the onion for 5–10 minutes, until lightly browned. Drain well and
put in the flan case. Beat the eggs, add the milk, seasoning, mustard and cheese, and
pour into the flan case. Bake in the oven at 200°C (400°F) mark 6 for 10 minutes.
Reduce the temperature to 180°C (350°F) mark 4 and bake the flan for a further
25 minutes or until the pastry is browned and the filling set. Serve hot or cold.

Serves 4

Pigeon pie

15 g ($\frac{1}{2}$ oz) butter
2 oven-ready pigeons
225 g (8 oz) carrots, trimmed, scrubbed and diced
2 medium onions, skinned and thinly sliced
400 ml ($\frac{3}{4}$ pint) chicken stock
(or stock made with the pigeon giblets)
15 ml (1 level tbsp) chopped fresh thyme
freshly ground sea salt and pepper
225 g (8 oz) flat mushrooms, wiped and thinly sliced
30 ml (2 level tbsp) chopped fresh parsley
175 g (6 oz) wholemeal pastry (see page 237)
milk or beaten egg to glaze

Melt the butter in a flameproof casserole, add the pigeons and brown them all over,
then remove from the pan. Add the carrots and onions to the pan, cover and sauté for
10 minutes until soft. Pour in the stock and bring to the boil. Add the thyme, replace the
pigeons and season well. Cover the casserole and bake in the oven at 180°C (350°F)
mark 4 for 1$\frac{1}{2}$ hours, until tender.

When the pigeons are cooked, remove them from the casserole. Remove all the meat
from the bones and dice it finely. Place the meat in a large pie dish with the mushrooms,
parsley and all the carrots, onions and cooking juices from the casserole.

Roll out the pastry and use to cover the pie dish. Decorate the top with any pastry
trimmings and brush with milk or beaten egg. Return the pie to the oven and bake at
200°C (400°F) mark 6 for 35 minutes until golden brown.

Serves 4

Stir-fried rice with seafood

Illustrated in colour opposite

1 egg
freshly ground sea salt and pepper
75 g (3 oz) butter
1 medium onion, skinned and chopped
15 ml (1 level tbsp) mild curry powder
225 g (8 oz) brown rice, cooked
50 g (2 oz) peanuts, toasted
350 g (12 oz) peeled prawns
450 g (1 lb) cooked mackerel, flaked
50 g (2 oz) seedless raisins
chopped fresh parsley to garnish

Whisk the egg lightly with 10 ml (2 tsp) water and season well. Melt 15 g ($\frac{1}{2}$ oz) of the butter in a small frying pan, tilting the pan so that the surface is evenly greased. Pour in the egg mixture, and gently stir with a fork, allowing the uncooked egg to flow to the sides to cook. Once the egg has set, stop stirring and cook the omelette for another minute until the under-side is golden brown. Keep the omelette warm.

Melt the remaining butter in a large frying pan and fry the onion for 5 minutes until soft. Stir in the curry powder, rice, peanuts, prawns, mackerel and raisins and adjust the seasoning. Stir-fry (see page 150) for 8 minutes until heated through, then spoon into a warm serving dish. Cut the omelette into strips and arrange on top. Sprinkle with parsley.

Serves 4

Baked liver and brown rice risotto

Illustrated in colour opposite

450 g (1 lb) lamb's liver, sliced
350 g (12 oz) even-sized onions (about 6)
25 g (1 oz) butter or vegetable margarine
15 ml (1 tbsp) sunflower oil
2 green peppers, seeded and sliced
225 g (8 oz) brown rice
10 ml (2 level tsp) paprika
600 ml (1 pint) chicken stock
150 ml ($\frac{1}{4}$ pint) white wine
freshly ground sea salt and pepper

Cut the liver into fork-size pieces. Skin and halve the onions lengthways. Heat the fat and oil in a large shallow flameproof casserole, add the liver and cook quickly until browned. Remove the liver from the pan using a slotted spoon. Add the onions and peppers and cook for about 10 minutes until browned, then remove from the pan. Stir the rice, paprika, stock, wine and seasoning into the pan and bring to the boil. Place the onions around the edge of the casserole and the liver and pepper in the centre. Cover and cook at 170°C (325°F) mark 3 for 1 hour until tender. Season before serving.

Serves 4

Chicken hot pot

Illustrated in colour opposite

225 g (8 oz) butter beans, soaked (see page 23)
1.4-kg (3-lb) oven-ready chicken
700 g (1½ lb) potatoes, peeled
225 g (8 oz) leeks, trimmed, sliced and washed
freshly ground sea salt and pepper
10 ml (2 level tsp) Dijon mustard
15 ml (1 level tbsp) tomato purée
400 ml (¾ pint) chicken stock
25 g (1 oz) butter or vegetable margarine
chopped fresh parsley to garnish

Drain the beans and cook in boiling water for about 1½ hours, until tender. Drain well. Bone and skin the chicken and cut the meat into 2.5-cm (1-inch) dice. Slice the potatoes into thick matchsticks.

Layer up the chicken, leeks, drained beans and one third of the potato sticks in a 2.4-litre (4½-pint) ovenproof dish, seasoning each layer with salt and pepper. Mix the mustard and tomato purée into the stock and pour over the chicken mixture. Top with the remaining potatoes and dot with fat. Cover and cook in the oven at 180°C (350°F) mark 4 for about 1 hour until the potatoes are tender. Uncover and return to the oven at 220°C (425°F) mark 7 for about 30 minutes, until the top is golden and crisp. Serve sprinkled with parsley.

Serves 4–6

Spanish omelette

25 g (1 oz) butter
1 green pepper, seeded and finely chopped
2 large onions, skinned and chopped
1 garlic clove, skinned and finely chopped
225 g (8 oz) cooked potato, diced
4 eggs
pinch of paprika
freshly ground sea salt and pepper
100 g (4 oz) Cheddar cheese, grated
chopped fresh parsley to garnish

Melt the butter in a frying pan. Add the pepper, onion and garlic and cook for about 8 minutes or until lightly browned. Add the potato and heat through.

Beat together the eggs and seasonings, pour into the pan and cook gently, without stirring, until the egg is set and the under-side golden. Sprinkle the cheese on top of the omelette and place the pan under the grill to brown the top. Sprinkle the omelette with parsley, cut into wedges and serve straight from the pan.

Serves 4

Beef with herb dumplings

450 g (1 lb) lean stewing steak
1 large onion, skinned and sliced
2 carrots, trimmed, scrubbed and sliced
2 sticks of celery, trimmed, washed and sliced
freshly ground sea salt and pepper
400 ml (¾ pint) beef stock
15 ml (1 tbsp) tamari sauce

For the dumplings
225 g (8 oz) cottage cheese
2 eggs
30 ml (2 level tbsp) chopped fresh mixed herbs
75 g (3 oz) plain wholemeal flour
freshly ground sea salt and pepper

Cut the meat into 2.5-cm (1-inch) cubes. Place the meat and vegetables in a flameproof casserole and season well. Pour in the stock and tamari sauce, bring to the boil and cover. Bake in the oven at 170°C (325°F) mark 3 for 2 hours until tender. For the dumplings, sieve the cottage cheese and beat in the eggs, herbs, flour and seasoning. Place eight spoonfuls of the dumpling mixture in the casserole. Cover and return to the oven for a further 25 minutes until the dumplings are risen and golden.

Serves 4

Barley-stuffed mackerel

100 g (4 oz) toasted barley flakes
100 g (4 oz) butter or vegetable margarine
1 small onion, skinned
grated rind and juice of 1 lemon
freshly ground sea salt and pepper
4 mackerel, cleaned and heads removed
lemon slices and watercress to garnish

Beat together the barley flakes and the fat. Finely chop the onion and add to the barley flake mixture with the lemon rind and juice and seasoning. Divide the stuffing into four and use to fill the fish. Place the fish in a lightly greased shallow ovenproof dish. Cover and bake in the oven at 180°C (350°F) mark 4 for 30 minutes, until tender. Garnish with lemon slices and watercress.

Serves 4

Aduki bean and beef bake

25 g (1 oz) butter
1 large onion, skinned and chopped
450 g (1 lb) lean minced beef
25 g (1 oz) plain wholemeal flour
300 ml ($\frac{1}{2}$ pint) beef stock
30 ml (2 level tbsp) tomato purée
175 g (6 oz) aduki beans, soaked (see page 23)
4 large tomatoes, skinned and chopped
freshly ground sea salt and pepper

For the sauce
25 g (1 oz) butter
25 g (1 oz) plain wholemeal flour
300 ml ($\frac{1}{2}$ pint) milk
1 egg
100 g (4 oz) Cheddar cheese, grated

Melt the butter in a large saucepan and sauté the onion for about 5 minutes until soft. Stir in the beef and cook, stirring, until just browned. Stir in the flour and cook for 2 minutes. Gradually stir in the stock and tomato purée. Drain the beans and add to the pan with the tomatoes and seasoning. Bring to the boil, then cover and simmer gently for 1 hour until the beans are tender. Turn into a 1.7-litre (3-pint) ovenproof casserole.

For the sauce, melt the butter in a pan, stir in the flour and cook for 2 minutes. Remove from the heat and gradually stir in the milk. Return to the heat and cook until boiling and thickened. Cook for 2 minutes more and remove from the heat. Beat the egg into the sauce with the cheese and pour over the beef mixture. Bake in the oven at 190°C (375°F) mark 5 for 30 minutes, until the top is golden brown.

Serves 4

Lemon chicken

1 garlic clove, skinned and crushed
freshly ground sea salt and pepper
45 ml (3 tbsp) olive oil
juice of 4 lemons
1 onion, skinned and grated
4 chicken portions, skinned

Mix the garlic, seasoning, olive oil, lemon juice and grated onion together in a bowl. Wash and dry the chicken pieces, place them in a shallow dish and pour over the marinade. Leave to marinate for 1–2 hours.

Line a grill pan with foil. Arrange the chicken pieces in the pan and pour over the marinade. Grill, basting frequently, under a medium heat for 30–40 minutes, or until the chicken is cooked through and tender. Serve with any remaining juices.

Serves 4

Bean and vegetable stew

175 g (6 oz) cannellini beans, soaked (see page 23)
750 ml (1¼ pints) chicken stock
freshly ground sea salt and pepper
25 g (1 oz) butter
225 g (8 oz) courgettes, trimmed and sliced
3 sticks of celery, trimmed, washed and sliced
1 medium onion, skinned and sliced
1 small red pepper, seeded and sliced
225 g (8 oz) aubergine, diced
150 ml (¼ pint) dry cider
10 ml (2 level tsp) chopped fresh thyme

Drain the beans and place in a pan with the stock and seasoning. Bring to the boil, cover and simmer for 1 hour, until the beans are tender but still firm. Melt the butter in a large deep frying pan and sauté the courgettes, celery, onion, pepper and aubergine, a few at a time, for 5–10 minutes until golden. Add the vegetables to the beans and stock. Add the cider and thyme, cover and simmer gently for 30 minutes, until the beans and vegetables are tender. Spoon into a heated serving dish.

Serves 4

Curried chicken salad

175 g (6 oz) brown rice
1 medium cauliflower, trimmed and washed
45 ml (3 tbsp) French dressing (see page 172)
150 ml (¼ pint) mayonnaise (see page 171)
30 ml (2 tbsp) milk
15 ml (1 level tbsp) curry powder
freshly ground sea salt and pepper
350 g (12 oz) cold cooked chicken, diced
1 green pepper, seeded and cut into strips
2 sticks of celery, trimmed, washed and chopped
1 small onion, skinned and finely sliced
1 lettuce, washed

Bring a saucepan of lightly salted water to the boil. Stir in the rice, cover and simmer for 40–45 minutes, until the rice is just tender. Drain, rinse with cold water to stop the cooking process and drain again. Leave to cool.

Divide the cauliflower into small florets and toss with the rice in the French dressing. Combine the mayonnaise, milk, curry powder, salt and pepper in a large bowl and stir in the chicken. Add the rice mixture, the green pepper, celery and onion and mix well together. Arrange the lettuce leaves on a serving plate and pile the chicken salad on top. Serve with a tomato salad.

Serves 4

Lamb with leeks

4 lean lamb chump chops
3 large leeks, trimmed, sliced and washed
75 g (3 oz) pot barley
freshly ground sea salt and pepper
1 sprig of fresh rosemary
600 ml (1 pint) chicken stock
chopped fresh parsley to garnish

Place the chops, leeks and barley in a casserole dish and season well. Add the rosemary and stock. Cover and bake in the oven at 170°C (325°F) mark 3 for 1½ hours until tender. Sprinkle with the chopped parsley.

Serves 4

Italian salami pizza

For the dough
10 ml (2 level tsp) dried yeast
150 ml (¼ pint) tepid milk
225 g (8 oz) plain wholemeal flour
pinch of freshly ground sea salt
50 g (2 oz) vegetable margarine
1 egg, beaten

For the topping
15 g (½ oz) vegetable margarine
1 medium onion, skinned and sliced
4 large tomatoes, skinned and sliced
100 g (4 oz) Italian salami, finely sliced
freshly ground sea salt and pepper
5 ml (1 level tsp) chopped fresh basil
175–225 g (6–8 oz) Mozzarella cheese, sliced

Sprinkle the yeast into the milk and leave in a warm place for about 15 minutes until frothy. Mix the flour and salt together in a large bowl. Rub the margarine into the flour until the mixture resembles fine breadcrumbs. Stir in the yeast mixture and egg, to form a fairly soft dough. Knead well on a lightly floured surface for 10 minutes until smooth. Place the dough in the bowl, cover with a clean tea towel and leave in a warm place for about 1 hour until doubled in size.

For the topping, melt the margarine in a saucepan and sauté the onion for 5 minutes until soft. Knead the dough a little and roll out on a lightly floured surface into a 23-cm (9-inch) round. Place on a lightly greased baking sheet and spread the onion over the top. Arrange alternate slices of tomato and salami over the onion, season well and sprinkle with basil. Cover with the sliced cheese and bake in the oven at 220°C (425°F) mark 7 for 25 minutes, until golden brown. Serve sliced hot or cold.

Serves 4

Chicken apricot pasta

175 g (6 oz) wholewheat pasta rings
25 g (1 oz) vegetable margarine
1 onion, skinned and sliced
1 small red pepper, seeded and chopped
25 g (1 oz) plain wholemeal flour
600 ml (1 pint) chicken stock
75 g (3 oz) dried apricots, soaked overnight
350 g (12 oz) cold cooked chicken
freshly ground sea salt and pepper
10 ml (2 tsp) Worcestershire sauce
chopped fresh parsley to garnish

Cook the pasta in boiling salted water for 15 minutes or until tender, drain well and keep warm. Meanwhile, melt the margarine in a saucepan and sauté the onion and pepper for 5 minutes until soft. Stir in the flour and cook for 2 minutes. Gradually stir in the stock and bring to the boil, stirring, to thicken. Drain and roughly chop the apricots and chicken, stir into the sauce, season well and add the Worcestershire sauce. Cover and simmer for 20 minutes. Add the pasta to the mixture and mix well. Spoon into a heated serving dish and sprinkle with parsley.

Serves 4

Beef beanpot

350 g (12 oz) lean chuck steak
1 green pepper, seeded and sliced
225 g (8 oz) small even-sized onions, skinned
225 g (8 oz) dried broad beans, soaked (see page 23)
15 ml (1 level tbsp) chopped fresh oregano
freshly ground sea salt and pepper
1 litre (1¾ pints) beef stock

Cut the meat into small cubes. Place the meat and pepper in a large saucepan with the onions. Drain the beans and add to the pan with the oregano and seasoning. Pour in the stock. Bring to the boil, cover the pan and simmer gently for about 2 hours or until the meat and beans are tender.

Serves 4

Creamed butter beans and bacon

225 g (8 oz) butter beans, soaked (see page 23)
225 g (8 oz) lean unsmoked bacon, rinded and chopped
50 g (2 oz) butter
1 medium onion, skinned and finely chopped
45 ml (3 level tbsp) plain wholemeal flour
300 ml ($\frac{1}{2}$ pint) milk
150 ml ($\frac{1}{4}$ pint) soured cream
freshly ground sea salt and pepper
bacon rolls and chopped fresh parsley to garnish

Drain the beans and cook in boiling water for $1\frac{1}{2}$ hours until tender. Drain and keep hot.

Fry the bacon in its own fat until crisp. Mix with the beans, spoon into an ovenproof serving dish and keep hot.

Melt the butter and fry the onion for about 5 minutes until soft. Stir in the flour and cook, stirring, for 2 minutes. Remove from the heat and gradually stir in the milk. Cook, stirring, until boiling and thickened. Add the soured cream and seasoning and heat gently without boiling. Pour the sauce over the bean and bacon mixture and garnish with bacon rolls and parsley.

Serves 4

Pot-au-feu

900 g (2 lb) lean beef (brisket, flank or silverside)
3 litres (5 pints) water
10 ml (2 level tsp) freshly ground sea salt
2 carrots, trimmed, scrubbed and sliced
1 turnip, trimmed, peeled and sliced
1 onion, skinned and quartered
1 parsnip, trimmed, peeled and quartered
2 small leeks, trimmed, washed and quartered
2 sticks of celery, trimmed, washed and quartered
25 g (1 oz) pot barley
bouquet garni
1 small cabbage, trimmed, washed and quartered

Tie the meat securely to keep it in one piece. Put it into a large saucepan with the water and salt. Cover and simmer gently for 1 hour.

Add all the vegetables (except the cabbage), the barley and the bouquet garni and cook for another hour. Put the cabbage into the pan and continue cooking for a further 30 minutes, or until the cabbage is tender. Strain, reserving the broth, and remove the bouquet garni.

Traditionally, the meat should be sliced and served with the vegetables. Serve the broth, sprinkled with parsley, as a starter.

Serves 4

Poacher's pie

1 oven-ready rabbit
2 potatoes, peeled and sliced
1 leek, trimmed, sliced and washed
3–4 rashers of lean unsmoked bacon, rinded and chopped
freshly ground sea salt and pepper
15 ml (1 level tbsp) chopped fresh parsley
7.5 ml (1½ level tsp) chopped fresh marjoram
7.5 ml (1½ level tsp) chopped fresh thyme
150 ml (¼ pint) chicken stock or water
350 g (12 oz) wholemeal pastry (see page 237)
beaten egg to glaze

Remove the meat from the bones of the rabbit and roughly chop it. Fill a 1.1-litre (2-pint) pie dish with layers of potato, leek, rabbit meat and bacon, sprinkling each layer with seasoning and herbs. Pour in the stock or water.

Roll out the pastry to measure about 2.5 cm (1 inch) larger than the rim of the dish. Cut a circle of dough from around the outer edge of the pastry and position it on the rim of the dish. Dampen the rim well, then fit the dough over the top of the dish. Crimp well to seal and use any pastry trimmings to decorate the top. Make a hole in the middle of the pastry to allow the steam to escape, and brush with beaten egg.

Bake in the oven at 200°C (400°F) mark 6 for 15 minutes, then reduce the temperature to 170°C (325°F) mark 3 and cook for 1 hour. If the pastry browns too quickly, cover with foil or brown paper for the final part of the cooking.

Serves 4

Black-eye bean and bacon risotto

225 g (8 oz) lean unsmoked bacon, rinded
1 medium onion, skinned and chopped
3 sticks of celery, trimmed, washed and chopped
100 g (4 oz) black-eye beans, soaked (see page 23)
900 ml (1½ pints) chicken stock
freshly ground sea salt and pepper
15 ml (1 level tbsp) chopped fresh basil
100 g (4 oz) brown rice
chopped fresh parsley to garnish

Scissor-snip the bacon into small pieces. Place in a wide, heavy-based pan or flameproof casserole and fry in its own fat for 2–3 minutes. Add the onion and celery to the bacon and fry quickly for 10 minutes, until golden. Drain the beans and stir in with the stock, seasoning and basil. Bring to the boil, cover and simmer for 30 minutes. Stir in the rice, cover and simmer for about 45 minutes, until the rice and beans are tender. Serve hot, sprinkled with parsley.

Serves 4

Stir-fried mung beans and eggs

8 eggs
30 ml (2 tbsp) tamari sauce
225 g (8 oz) mung bean sprouts
60 ml (4 tbsp) sunflower oil
1 large green pepper, seeded and chopped
100 g (4 oz) mushrooms, wiped and chopped
2 medium onions, skinned and chopped
1 garlic clove, skinned and finely chopped

Beat the eggs with the tamari sauce. Rinse the bean sprouts and remove the tough green casings. Heat the oil in a large frying pan and add the bean sprouts, pepper, mushrooms, onions and garlic and stir for 1 minute. Pour in the eggs and cook, folding the mixture continuously, until the eggs are set.

Serves 4

Chicken in a brick with cheese pasta

1 garlic clove, skinned and crushed
1.4-kg (3-lb) oven-ready chicken
$\frac{1}{2}$ a lemon
a few sprigs of parsley
freshly ground sea salt and pepper
15 ml (1 tbsp) olive oil
chopped fresh parsley to garnish

For the pasta sauce
225 g (8 oz) wholewheat macaroni
100 g (4 oz) Dolcelatte cheese
25 g (1 oz) butter
150 ml ($\frac{1}{4}$ pint) soured cream
25 g (1 oz) cashew nuts, toasted and finely chopped
grated rind and juice of $\frac{1}{2}$ a lemon

Place the garlic inside the chicken with the lemon half and parsley sprigs. Season the chicken inside and out. Place in a chicken brick and brush with oil. Cover with the lid and place in a cold oven. Turn the oven on at 240°C (475°F) mark 9 and bake the chicken for $1\frac{1}{2}$ hours until tender.

Meanwhile, 30 minutes before the end of the cooking time, make the pasta sauce. Cook the macaroni in boiling salted water for 15 minutes, until tender. Crumble the cheese into a bowl with the butter, stand the bowl over a saucepan of hot water and heat until melted. Stir in the soured cream and heat gently for a further 5 minutes, then add the nuts with the lemon rind and juice.

Drain the macaroni and stir into the sauce. Place the chicken on a heated serving dish and surround with the pasta. Sprinkle with chopped parsley.

Serves 4

115

Bean-stuffed cabbage rolls

75 g (3 oz) foule beans, soaked (see page 23)
175 g (6 oz) garlic sausage, finely chopped
75 g (3 oz) butter
2 medium tomatoes, skinned and chopped
1 medium onion, skinned and chopped
15 ml (1 level tbsp) tomato purée
freshly ground sea salt and pepper
8 large cabbage leaves, *eg.* Savoy
30 ml (2 level tbsp) chopped fresh parsley

Drain the beans and cook in boiling water for about $1\frac{1}{4}$ hours until very tender. Drain and mix in the garlic sausage. Heat 25 g (1 oz) of the butter in a pan and sauté the tomatoes and onion for about 5 minutes until soft. Add to the bean mixture with the tomato purée and seasoning.

Wash the cabbage leaves and trim out any tough centre stalks, blanch in boiling salted water for about 4 minutes, then drain. Divide the bean stuffing between the leaves, roll up securely and place in a buttered ovenproof dish. Cover closely with foil and bake in the oven at 180°C (350°F) mark 4 for 30–35 minutes.

Beat the remaining butter with a wooden spoon to soften, then mix in the parsley. Serve the cabbage rolls topped with dabs of parsley butter.

Serves 4

Smothered mackerel

4 fresh mackerel, cleaned and heads removed
1 large onion, skinned and sliced
2 tomatoes, skinned and sliced
grated rind and juice of 1 lemon
freshly ground sea salt and pepper
1 bay leaf
15 ml (1 level tbsp) chopped fresh parsley
2.5 ml ($\frac{1}{2}$ level tsp) ground mace

Place the fish in an ovenproof dish and cover with the onion and tomatoes. Add the remaining ingredients and cover the dish. Bake in the oven at 190°C (375°F) mark 5 for 30 minutes. Uncover and cook for a further 10 minutes until the fish are tender.

Serves 4

Cheese-stuffed aubergines

4 medium aubergines
15 g ($\frac{1}{2}$ oz) vegetable margarine
2 medium onions, skinned and chopped
50 g (2 oz) mushrooms, wiped
450 g (1 lb) Cheddar cheese, grated
60 ml (4 level tbsp) chopped fresh chives
freshly ground sea salt and pepper
100 g (4 oz) fresh wholemeal breadcrumbs
chopped fresh parsley to garnish

Cut the aubergines in half lengthways. Scoop out and roughly chop the flesh and sprinkle the flesh and shells with salt. Leave for 30 minutes to drain off excess juice, then rinse off the salt.

Melt the margarine in a saucepan and sauté the onion and aubergine flesh for about 5 minutes, until soft. Roughly chop the mushrooms, add to the onion and aubergine mixture and cook for a further 2 minutes. Remove from the heat, stir in 350 g (12 oz) of the cheese and the chives, and season well. Spoon the filling into the aubergine shells.

Mix together the remaining cheese and the breadcrumbs and sprinkle over the top. Place on a baking sheet and bake in the oven at 180°C (350°F) mark 4 for 45 minutes until the topping is golden brown. Serve garnished with parsley.

Serves 4

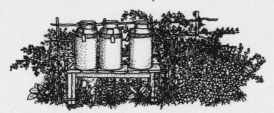

Oven-baked spaghetti

225 g (8 oz) wholewheat spaghetti
50 g (2 oz) butter
225 g (8 oz) mushrooms, wiped and sliced
2 tomatoes, skinned and chopped
freshly ground sea salt and pepper
50 g (2 oz) Cheddar or Cheshire cheese, grated

Cook the spaghetti in boiling salted water for about 10 minutes until just soft. Drain and set aside.

Melt the butter in a pan and gently fry the mushrooms for 2–3 minutes until soft. Mix the tomatoes with the mushrooms in the pan, then stir this mixture into the spaghetti. Season with salt and pepper, then pile into the casserole. Cover with the cheese and bake in the oven at 190°C (375°F) mark 5 for 30 minutes or until the cheese is melted and beginning to brown.

Serves 4

Smoky bean salad

175 g (6 oz) butter beans, soaked (see page 23)
freshly ground sea salt
450 g (1 lb) smoked haddock
1 lettuce, washed
1 hard-boiled egg, sliced, to garnish

For the dressing
45 ml (3 tbsp) natural yogurt
15–30 ml (1–2 tbsp) lemon juice
15 ml (1 level tbsp) chopped fresh parsley
1.25 ml ($\frac{1}{4}$ level tsp) curry powder
freshly ground pepper

Drain the beans and put them in a saucepan. Cover the beans with water and bring to the boil. Reduce the heat and simmer, covered, for $1\frac{1}{2}$ hours, or until the beans are tender. Season with salt just before the end of the cooking time. Drain and leave to cool.

Put the haddock into a bowl or jug and pour over boiling water to cover. Leave for 10–15 minutes or until the fish is cooked and slightly flaky. Drain and flake with a fork, removing any bones. When both the beans and fish are cold, combine them in a bowl.

To make the dressing, blend the yogurt and lemon juice together and gradually beat in the parsley, curry powder and pepper. Carefully stir this dressing into the bean mixture. Arrange the lettuce leaves on a serving plate, pile the bean mixture on top and garnish with egg slices.

Serves 4

Spaghetti alla carbonara

350 g (12 oz) wholewheat spaghetti
4 eggs
45 ml (3 level tbsp) grated Parmesan cheese
75 g (3 oz) Cheddar cheese, grated
freshly ground sea salt and pepper
225 g (8 oz) lean unsmoked bacon, rinded
150 ml ($\frac{1}{4}$ pint) soured cream
45 ml (3 level tbsp) chopped fresh parsley

Cook the spaghetti in boiling salted water for 15 minutes, until tender. Meanwhile, beat together the eggs, 30 ml (2 level tbsp) Parmesan cheese and 50 g (2 oz) of Cheddar cheese and season well. Chop the bacon and fry in its own fat until crisp. Remove from the heat and stir in the soured cream. Heat very gently without boiling.

When the spaghetti is cooked, drain well, then return the spaghetti to the pan. Add the egg and cheese mixture and toss together. (The heat of the spaghetti will cook the eggs.) Stir in 30 ml (2 level tbsp) of the parsley and the bacon mixture. Spoon into a heated serving dish and sprinkle with the remaining cheese and parsley.

Serves 4

Savoury haddock crumble

450 g (1 lb) haddock
300 ml (½ pint) milk
freshly ground sea salt and pepper
2 hard-boiled eggs, chopped
1 medium onion, skinned and chopped
15 g (½ oz) vegetable margarine
15 g (½ oz) plain wheatmeal flour
chopped fresh parsley to garnish

For the topping
25 g (1 oz) vegetable margarine
75 g (3 oz) plain wheatmeal flour
25 g (1 oz) rolled oats

Place the haddock, milk and seasoning in a saucepan and simmer gently for 10–15 minutes until the haddock is tender. Drain, reserving the milk, and skin and flake the fish. Place the haddock, egg and onion in a shallow ovenproof dish.

Melt the margarine in a saucepan, stir in the flour and cook for 1–2 minutes. Remove from the heat. Make the reserved milk up to 300 ml (½ pint) with a little more milk, if necessary, and gradually stir into the flour mixture. Bring to the boil, stirring, and cook for a further 1–2 minutes until thick. Season, then stir into the fish mixture.

To make the crumble topping, rub the margarine into the flour until the mixture resembles breadcrumbs, then stir in the oats. Sprinkle the topping over the fish mixture and bake in the oven at 190°C (375°F) mark 5 for 20 minutes until golden brown. Garnish with chopped parsley.

Serves 4

Fennel bake

450 g (1 lb) potatoes, peeled
1 medium head of fennel, trimmed and halved
freshly ground sea salt and pepper
2 eggs
150 ml (¼ pint) milk
100 g (4 oz) lean unsmoked bacon, rinded and diced
100 g (4 oz) wholemeal bread, diced
50 g (2 oz) Cheddar cheese, grated

Cook the potatoes and fennel in boiling salted water for 15 minutes until just tender, then drain well. Thinly slice the potatoes and fennel, arrange in an ovenproof casserole and season well.

Beat together the eggs and milk and pour over the vegetables. Sprinkle over the bacon and bread pieces and top with grated cheese. Bake in the oven at 190°C (375°F) mark 5 for 45–50 minutes, until the vegetables are tender and the top golden.

Serves 4

Leeks with hazelnut sauce

8 leeks, trimmed and washed
25 g (1 oz) butter
25 g (1 oz) plain wholemeal flour
400 ml ($\frac{3}{4}$ pint) milk
freshly ground sea salt and pepper
25 g (1 oz) hazelnuts, blanched, skinned and chopped
8 slices of lean ham
100 g (4 oz) Cheddar cheese, grated
parsley sprigs to garnish

Place the leeks in a pan of boiling salted water and cook for 15 minutes until tender. Meanwhile, melt the butter in a saucepan, stir in the flour and cook for 1–2 minutes. Remove the pan from the heat and gradually stir in the milk and seasoning. Return to the heat and stir continuously until the sauce boils and thickens. Simmer for a further 2–3 minutes, then add the chopped hazelnuts.

Drain the leeks and wrap each one in a slice of ham. Arrange the leek and ham rolls in a flameproof serving dish and cover with sauce. Sprinkle with cheese and grill until the cheese melts and starts to brown. Garnish with sprigs of parsley.

Serves 4

Fish and cider casserole

700 g (1$\frac{1}{2}$ lb) cod or haddock fillets
2 medium onions, skinned and finely chopped
225 g (8 oz) tomatoes, skinned and sliced
150 ml ($\frac{1}{4}$ pint) dry cider
10 ml (2 level tsp) chopped fresh sage or mixed herbs
freshly ground sea salt and pepper
30–45 ml (2–3 level tbsp) fresh wholemeal breadcrumbs
25 g (1 oz) Cheddar cheese, grated

Cut each fillet in half and place in an ovenproof casserole. Scatter the onions and tomatoes over and pour the cider round the fish. Sprinkle with the herbs and seasoning, cover and bake in the oven at 170°C (325°F) mark 3 for 20–30 minutes, until the fish is cooked and slightly flaky. Remove the lid, sprinkle the fish with the breadcrumbs and cheese and brown under a hot grill before serving.

Serves 4

Carrot nut burgers

40 g (1½ oz) butter
40 g (1½ oz) plain wholemeal flour
300 ml (½ pint) chicken stock
freshly ground sea salt and pepper
2 carrots, trimmed and scrubbed
30 ml (2 level tbsp) chopped fresh chives
225 g (8 oz) fresh wholemeal breadcrumbs
50 g (2 oz) mixed nuts, chopped
plain wholemeal flour for coating
1 egg, beaten
parsley sprigs to garnish

Melt the butter in a saucepan, add the flour and cook for 2 minutes. Gradually stir in the stock, bring to the boil, stirring, to thicken and season well. Grate the carrots finely and stir into the sauce with the chives, 100 g (4 oz) of the breadcrumbs and the nuts. Mix well and leave to cool.

Divide the mixture into four and shape into burgers. Coat with wholemeal flour. Place in the freezing compartment of the refrigerator for 20 minutes until firm.

Dip the burgers in beaten egg, then coat with the remaining breadcrumbs. Place on a baking sheet. Bake in the oven at 180°C (300°F) mark 4 for 30 minutes until deep golden. Garnish with sprigs of parsley and serve with tomato sauce (see page 185).

Serves 4

Vegetable and egg risotto

15 ml (1 tbsp) vegetable oil
1 medium onion, skinned and chopped
175 g (6 oz) brown rice
600 ml (1 pint) vegetable stock
15 ml (1 tbsp) tamari sauce
freshly ground sea salt and pepper
75 g (3 oz) mushrooms, wiped and sliced
175 g (6 oz) mung bean sprouts
50 g (2 oz) peanuts, toasted
4 hard-boiled eggs, roughly chopped
chopped fresh parsley to garnish

Heat the oil in a large frying pan and sauté the onion for 5 minutes until soft. Add the rice and cook for a further 1 minute. Stir in the stock and tamari sauce and season well. Cover and simmer gently for 40–45 minutes, until the rice is just tender.

Stir the mushrooms into the rice with the bean sprouts, nuts and eggs. Stir-fry (see page 150) for 8 minutes, until the mushrooms are just tender and the bean sprouts still crisp. Spoon into a heated serving dish and sprinkle with parsley.

Serves 4

Chilli sausage casserole
Illustrated in colour opposite

100 g (4 oz) red kidney beans, soaked (see page 23)
450 g (1 lb) sausagemeat
5 ml (1 level tsp) each of chopped fresh rosemary, sage, thyme
5 ml (1 level tsp) paprika
15 ml (1 tbsp) sunflower oil
450 g (1 lb) green cabbage, trimmed and shredded
1 large onion, skinned and sliced
15 ml (1 level tbsp) chilli seasoning
30 ml (2 level tbsp) plain wholemeal flour
1 garlic clove, skinned and crushed
150 ml ($\frac{1}{4}$ pint) red wine
400 ml ($\frac{3}{4}$ pint) beef stock
15 ml (1 level tbsp) tomato purée
15 ml (1 level tbsp) demerara sugar
freshly ground sea salt and pepper

Drain the beans and cook in boiling water for about 1 hour, until tender, then drain well. Place the sausagemeat in a bowl and work in the herbs and paprika. With well-floured hands, roll the mixture into sixteen balls the size of golf balls. Heat the oil in a frying pan and fry the sausage balls until lightly browned, then drain well on absorbent kitchen paper.

In a shallow 1.7-litre (3-pint) casserole, layer up the cabbage, onion, beans and sausage balls. Blend the chilli seasoning, flour and garlic into the pan residue, adding more oil if necessary, and cook for 1 minute. Stir in the wine, stock, tomato purée, sugar and seasoning and bring to the boil. Pour over the ingredients in the casserole. Cover and bake in the oven at 180°C (350°F) mark 4 for about 1 hour, until tender.

Serves 6

Nutty cheese bake
175 g (6 oz) mixed nuts, finely chopped
225 g (8 oz) Cheshire cheese
4 large tomatoes, skinned and chopped
3 eggs
freshly ground sea salt and pepper
30 ml (2 level tbsp) chopped fresh parsley

Put the nuts in a bowl, crumble in the cheese and mix in the tomatoes. Beat the eggs with the seasoning and parsley and stir into the mixture. Grease an ovenproof dish and pour in the nut mixture. Bake in the oven at 200°C (400°F) mark 6 for about 30 minutes, until golden brown.

Serves 6

Chicken pot-roast with walnuts

Illustrated in colour opposite

1.6-kg (3½-lb) oven-ready chicken
25 g (1 oz) butter or vegetable margarine
15 ml (1 tbsp) sunflower oil
350 g (12 oz) celery, trimmed, washed and sliced
200 g (7 oz) carrots, trimmed, scrubbed and cut into chunks
200 g (7 oz) leeks, trimmed, sliced and washed
50 g (2 oz) button mushrooms, wiped
25 g (1 oz) walnut halves

For the stuffing
15 g (½ oz) butter or vegetable margarine
½ a small onion, skinned and finely chopped
25 g (1 oz) mushrooms, wiped and finely chopped
30 ml (2 level tbsp) chopped walnuts
25 g (1 oz) fresh wholemeal breadcrumbs
5 ml (1 level tsp) chopped fresh parsley
1 egg, size 6, beaten
freshly ground sea salt and pepper

For the stuffing, melt the fat in a pan, add the onion and mushrooms and fry gently for about 5 minutes, until just soft. Stir in the walnuts, breadcrumbs and parsley with enough beaten egg to bind. Season with salt and pepper. Use to stuff the neck cavity of the chicken and truss.

Melt the fat and the sunflower oil in a frying pan and fry the chicken until brown on all sides. Remove and place in a deep ovenproof casserole. Sauté the prepared vegetables and the walnut halves in the remaining fat until lightly browned, then drain and add them to the chicken in the casserole. Cover and cook in the oven at 150°C (300°F) mark 2 for about 2 hours, until tender.

Serves 6

Savoury lamb and mushrooms

2 medium onions, skinned and sliced
3 tomatoes, skinned and sliced
100 g (4 oz) mushrooms, wiped and sliced
4 lamb chops, trimmed of fat
butter or vegetable margarine
freshly ground sea salt and pepper

Place the onions, tomatoes and mushrooms in an ovenproof dish. Arrange the chops on top of the vegetables, place a knob of fat on each and season with salt and pepper. Cook in the oven at 200°C (400°F) mark 6 for 45 minutes or until the chops are tender.

Serves 4

Special Occasion Dishes

Impressive special occasion food does not have to mean unhealthy food and, just because you have invited friends for a dinner party, you do not have to lapse from your wholefood style of eating.

When you are planning a special dinner, the first thing to remember is not to worry over whether your guests are going to enjoy your spread of natural foods. Everyone likes something different when they go out and, besides, wholefood tastes so much better than processed or over-rich food that it will not fail to impress, however simple or elaborate your dishes may be. Do not apologise for your 'funny way' of eating or go to the opposite extreme and tell your guests that this is the *only* way to eat. Just serve up in a perfectly natural way and watch how your meal is enjoyed. Many an unsuspecting guest has first become interested in wholefoods in this way.

WHAT TO SERVE The more conventional style of meal with a main dish and side dishes such as vegetables and salads is probably the best for entertaining. You will probably

want to have both a first course or a soup and a dessert, so keep your cooking methods and your dishes quite light in order to avoid that over-full feeling at the end of the meal.

On some occasions your dinner-party food can be exactly the same as you would give to your family every day, but there are times which call for something really special. The more expensive cuts of meat are still looked on as the most impressive, but you can also achieve great results with meat such as shoulder of lamb or a chicken, provided they are given the right treatment and accompaniments.

If you really want to splash out, game is a good choice for a wholefood dinner party since it is the most naturally produced of all meats. Partridge and grouse can be very expensive, but the occasional brace of pheasants should be within most people's price range; and don't forget pigeons, which are very cheap and available all the year round. Both these birds will be best if you can buy them on the feather and hang and pluck them yourself. Hare, too, can be quite economical and in some supermarkets you can buy joints of hare or the diced meat.

Game is so delicious that it can be roasted plain and still make a perfect dinner-party dish and, to accompany it, you can make a wholemeal bread sauce (see page 185). If you want a cold meal then the meat can be diced and made into a salad. Older game is best casseroled or braised, and it can be tenderised a great deal if you marinate it first.

Fish is very often neglected when it comes to special occasion meals, but it can be just as impressive as meat. The more usual kinds such as cod can be given garnishes and sauces; or you can choose less common fish such as halibut and mullet.

When serving dinner-party meals, garnish them prettily with chopped parsley, twists of lemon or cucumber, thin slices of tomato or small bunches of watercress or alfalfa. Make the table look attractive with a bowl of fresh fruit for a centrepiece, beside which you can put a basket of home-made wholemeal rolls.

With good food and good company your dinner party is sure to be a success.

Pigeons roasted in foil

4 oven-ready pigeons
4 sage leaves
4 small savory sprigs
50 g (2 oz) butter or 60 ml (4 tbsp) olive oil
freshly ground black pepper

Inside each pigeon place a sage leaf and a sprig of savory. Truss the pigeons, then either spread them with butter or brush them with oil and season the outsides with pepper. Wrap each pigeon in a piece of foil, stand the parcels on a baking sheet and bake in the oven at 180°C (350°F) mark 4 for $1\frac{1}{2}$ hours or until the pigeons are tender.

Serve the pigeons still wrapped in foil and unwrap them on individual plates to prevent any of the juices escaping. The pigeons are best served quite plainly, without any additional sauce or gravy, and with a salad to accompany them.

Serves 4

Vegetable stuffed chicken

1 medium carrot, trimmed and scrubbed
2 sticks of celery, trimmed and washed
1 small onion, skinned
175 g (6 oz) swede, peeled
½ a small red pepper, seeded
25 g (1 oz) almonds, toasted
freshly ground sea salt and pepper
75 ml (5 tbsp) white wine
1.6-kg (3½-lb) chicken, boned
watercress to garnish

Grate the carrot, celery, onion and swede into a bowl. Chop the pepper and nuts and mix into the vegetables. Season with salt and pepper and bind together with the wine.

Lay the chicken out flat, skin side down, and place the stuffing in the centre. Fold the sides of the chicken over the stuffing to enclose it and secure with metal skewers. Weigh the chicken and place, join side down, on a wire rack over a roasting tin. Roast for 20 minutes per 450 g (1 lb), plus 20 minutes, at 190°C (375°F) mark 5, until golden brown. Serve sliced, garnished with watercress.

Serves 6

Chilli con carne

350 g (12 oz) red kidney beans, soaked (see page 23)
15 ml (1 tbsp) olive oil
1 large onion, skinned and chopped
1 garlic clove, skinned and crushed
700 g (1½ lb) lean minced beef
4 tomatoes, skinned
1 green pepper, seeded
30 ml (2 level tbsp) tomato purée
15 ml (1 tbsp) red wine vinegar
400 ml (¾ pint) beef stock
5 ml (1 level tsp) demerara sugar
15 ml (1 level tbsp) paprika
5–10 ml (1–2 level tsp) chilli powder

Drain the beans and place in a saucepan of water. Bring to the boil, cover and simmer for 1 hour or until tender.

Heat the oil in a large saucepan and sauté the onion and garlic for 5 minutes until soft. Add the meat and cook until lightly browned. Chop the tomatoes and green pepper and stir into the beef with the remaining ingredients. Cover and simmer gently for 30 minutes until tender. Drain the beans, add them to the beef and vegetable mixture and cook for a further 10 minutes.

Serves 6

Beef couscous

700 g (1½ lb) lean stewing steak
1 large onion, skinned and sliced
2 red peppers, seeded and sliced
450 g (1 lb) courgettes, washed, trimmed and sliced
1 medium aubergine, washed, trimmed and diced
450 g (1 lb) tomatoes, skinned and chopped
1.1 litres (2 pints) beef stock
freshly ground sea salt and pepper
10 ml (2 level tsp) paprika
5 ml (1 level tsp) cumin
30 ml (2 level tbsp) tomato purée
450 g (1 lb) couscous
400 ml (¾ pint) tepid water
75 g (3 oz) butter

Cut the meat into cubes and place with all the vegetables in a large saucepan. Add the stock, seasoning, spices and tomato purée. Bring to the boil, cover and simmer gently for 1½ hours.

After 30 minutes place the couscous in a large bowl with the water and leave to soak for 1 hour. Drain the couscous grains and put them in a steamer over the beef stew. Cover and simmer for a further 40 minutes until the meat is tender. Remove the steamer and cover the saucepan. Place the couscous in a large mixing bowl. Melt the butter and beat it into the couscous with 50 ml (2 fl oz) salt water. Leave to stand for 15 minutes, then stir the couscous well to remove any lumps. Return to the steamer over the saucepan, cover and steam for another 20 minutes until the couscous is light and fluffy. Serve the beef stew and couscous separately in warm serving dishes.

Serves 6

Pork with black beans and orange

450 g (1 lb) lean blade of pork, diced
1 large onion, skinned and sliced
225 g (8 oz) carrots, trimmed, scrubbed and sliced
900 ml (1½ pints) chicken stock
1 bay leaf
grated rind and juice of 1 small orange
225 g (8 oz) black beans, soaked (see page 23)
freshly ground sea salt and pepper

Place the meat and vegetables in a large saucepan and add the stock, bay leaf and grated orange rind and juice. Drain the beans and add to the pan. Season well with salt and pepper, cover and simmer for about 1½ hours, until all is tender. Remove the bay leaf before serving.

Serves 4

Beef curry

450 g (1 lb) lean stewing steak
15 ml (1 tbsp) sunflower oil
1 large onion, skinned and chopped
1 cooking apple, peeled, cored and chopped
15 ml (1 level tbsp) curry powder
25 g (1 oz) plain wholemeal flour
400 ml ($\frac{3}{4}$ pint) beef stock
25 g (1 oz) seedless raisins
25 g (1 oz) flaked almonds
2 tomatoes, skinned and chopped
15 ml (1 level tbsp) desiccated coconut
juice of $\frac{1}{2}$ a lemon
15 ml (1 level tbsp) mango chutney

Cut the meat into 2-cm ($\frac{3}{4}$-inch) cubes. Heat the oil in a large saucepan, add the onion and beef and cook for 10 minutes until brown. Add the apple, curry powder and flour and cook for 2 minutes. Gradually stir in the stock and cook for 1–2 minutes until the mixture thickens. Stir in the remaining ingredients. Cover and simmer gently for 1$\frac{1}{2}$ hours until the meat is tender. Serve with puris (see page 180) or brown rice.

Serves 4

Cherry-glazed duck

2.3-kg (5-lb) oven-ready duck
450 g (1 lb) cherries
300 ml ($\frac{1}{2}$ pint) dry white wine

Prick the duck all over with a needle or very fine skewer and place on a wire rack in a roasting tin. Roast in the oven at 200°C (400°F) mark 6 for about 1$\frac{3}{4}$ hours, until tender and golden brown. Reserve twelve of the cherries and simmer the remainder in the wine until tender, then sieve to remove the stones and skin. Spoon some of this cherry sauce over the duck 20 minutes before the cooking time is completed and baste again 10 minutes later. Boil the remaining mixture vigorously to reduce the amount by half. Serve the duck on a large dish with the whole cherries and the remaining cherry sauce.

Serves 4

Devilled poussins

4 oven-ready poussins
a little cayenne pepper
2.5 ml ($\frac{1}{2}$ level tsp) freshly ground black pepper
15 ml (1 tbsp) Worcestershire sauce
15 ml (1 level tbsp) prepared mustard
15 ml (1 tbsp) cider vinegar
60 ml (4 tbsp) sunflower oil

Line a grill pan with foil. Split the birds down the back and open them out. Blend all the remaining ingredients together until smooth. Arrange the poussins in the lined grill pan and spoon over the mixture. Cook under a medium heat, turning them once or twice, for about 20 minutes or until the meat is cooked through and tender. Baste the meat with the devilled juices once or twice during cooking.

Serves 4

Eastern style lamb cutlets

8 lamb cutlets, trimmed of fat
300 ml ($\frac{1}{2}$ pint) natural yogurt
5 ml (1 level tsp) curry powder
10 ml (2 level tsp) chopped mixed fresh herbs
1 garlic clove, skinned and crushed
chopped fresh parsley to garnish

Place the cutlets in a single layer in a shallow ovenproof dish and prick them with a skewer. Blend together the yogurt, curry powder, herbs and garlic, and spoon over the lamb. Leave, covered, in the refrigerator for 24 hours.

Just before cooking, baste the cutlets with the yogurt mixture. Cook in the oven, uncovered, at 190°C (375°F) mark 5 for about 1 hour or until the lamb is cooked and tender. Baste occasionally during the cooking period. Garnish with chopped parsley and serve with plain brown rice.

Serves 4

Almond chicken

4 chicken portions, skinned
1 egg, beaten
100 g (4 oz) ground almonds
50 g (2 oz) butter

Brush the chicken portions with egg and roll them in the ground almonds, pressing them in well. Melt the butter in a shallow roasting tin and add the chicken pieces. Roast in the oven at 200°C (400°F) mark 6 for 45 minutes–1 hour or until the meat is tender. Baste once or twice during cooking. Serve with a green or mixed salad.

Serves 4

Oriental chicken

4 chicken portions, skinned
juice of 1 lemon
freshly ground sea salt and pepper
15 ml (1 tbsp) tamari sauce
350 ml (12 fl oz) chicken stock
20 ml (4 level tsp) cornflour
½ a fresh pineapple, peeled, trimmed and diced
25 g (1 oz) blanched almonds, toasted

Line a grill pan with foil. Sprinkle the chicken pieces with the lemon juice and season with salt and pepper. Arrange the chicken in the grill pan and grill under a medium heat for 20–25 minutes or until the pieces are cooked through and tender.

Add the tamari sauce to the stock and heat to boiling point. Mix the cornflour to a smooth paste with a little water then stir into the stock and add the pineapple pieces. Simmer for 5–10 minutes. Transfer the chicken to a heated serving dish and pour over the pineapple sauce. Serve sprinkled with the toasted almonds.

Serves 4

Jugged hare

1 hare, skinned and jointed
25 g (1 oz) vegetable margarine
50 g (2 oz) lean unsmoked bacon, rinded and chopped
2 cloves
1 medium onion, skinned
1 carrot, trimmed, scrubbed and sliced
1 stick of celery, trimmed, washed and sliced
about 900 ml (1½ pints) chicken stock
bouquet garni
juice of ½ a lemon
45 ml (3 level tbsp) plain wholemeal flour
15 ml (1 level tbsp) redcurrant jelly
100 ml (4 fl oz) port or red wine (optional)

Ask your butcher to collect 300 ml (½ pint) of hare's blood and to include this with the joints. Melt the margarine in a flameproof casserole and add the bacon and hare joints. Cook for 5–8 minutes or until the joints are browned. Push the cloves into the onion and add all the vegetables to the casserole with enough stock to cover the joints. Add the bouquet garni and lemon juice. Cover and cook in the oven at 170°C (325°F) mark 3 for 3–3½ hours, or until the meat is tender.

A few minutes before serving, blend the flour with a little cold water to a smooth cream, stir in the hare's blood and add to the casserole with the jelly and wine (if used). Remove the bouquet garni and cloves, reheat the casserole without boiling and serve with redcurrant jelly.

Serves 4

Lamb pot roast with bean stuffing

225 g (8 oz) rose cocoa beans, soaked (see page 23)
30 ml (2 tbsp) chopped fresh mint
60 ml (4 level tbsp) fresh wholemeal breadcrumbs
1 egg, beaten
freshly ground sea salt and pepper
2–2.3-kg (4½–5-lb) leg of lamb, boned
300 ml (½ pint) chicken stock
60 ml (4 level tbsp) plain wholemeal flour

Drain the beans and divide by weighing into two halves. Cook one half in gently boiling water for about 1 hour until tender. Drain and mash the cooked beans lightly with the back of a wooden spoon and mix them with half the mint, the breadcrumbs, beaten egg and seasoning. Use to stuff the meat cavity and tie securely. Cook any left-over stuffing separately.

Place the meat in a large flameproof dish and put the remaining beans round it. Add the stock and the remaining mint and bring to the boil. Cover and cook in the oven at 150°C (300°F) mark 2 for 3–3½ hours, or until the meat and beans are tender.

Pour off the juice and keep the meat and beans warm. Pour a little of the juice into a saucepan and blend in the wholemeal flour to form a paste. Gradually add the rest of the juice and heat, stirring continuously, until the gravy thickens. Adjust the seasoning.

Serve the lamb with the beans and serve the gravy separately.

Serves 6

Curried pork chops with apples and raisins

45 ml (3 tbsp) olive or sunflower oil
1 garlic clove, skinned and crushed
freshly ground sea salt
15 ml (1 level tbsp) curry powder
2 small cooking apples, peeled and cored
4 pork loin chops, trimmed of fat
60 ml (4 level tbsp) finely chopped onion
25 g (1 oz) seedless raisins

Whisk together the oil, garlic, salt and curry powder, and cut the apples into 0.5-cm (¼-inch) slices. Brush one side of the chops with half the curry mixture. Put the chops, brushed side down, in a grill pan and brush the other side with the remaining curry mixture. Grill the chops under a high heat until the first side is golden brown, turn them over and scatter them with the chopped onion. Return to the heat until the onion is brown. Lay two or three apple rings (depending on their size) on each chop and fill the centres of the rings with raisins. Put the pan back under the grill and cook until the apple rings are just beginning to brown.

Serves 4

Lamb with cheese stuffing

1 small onion, skinned and finely chopped
1 small cooking apple, peeled, cored and grated
75 g (3 oz) Red Leicester cheese, grated
50 g (2 oz) fresh wholemeal breadcrumbs
1 egg, beaten
grated rind and juice of $\frac{1}{2}$ a small lemon
freshly ground sea salt and pepper
2.3-kg (5-lb) leg of lamb, boned
watercress to garnish

Mix together the onion, apple, cheese, breadcrumbs, egg, lemon rind and juice and seasoning. Fill the lamb cavity with this stuffing and secure the open end with skewers or sew up with string.

Weigh the joint and roast in the oven for 25 minutes per 450 g (1 lb), plus 25 minutes, at 190°C (375°F) mark 5 until tender. Cook any remaining stuffing around the joint in the roasting tin. Serve garnished with watercress.

Serves 6

Lamb and apricot kebabs

700 g (1½ lb) boned lean shoulder of lamb
60 ml (4 tbsp) olive oil
juice of 1 lemon
1 garlic clove, skinned and crushed
pinch of freshly ground sea salt
5 ml (1 level tsp) ground cumin
5 ml (1 level tsp) ground coriander
pinch of cayenne pepper
12 apricots
2 large onions, skinned

Cut the lamb into 2.5-cm (1-inch) cubes. In a large bowl, whisk together the oil, lemon juice, garlic, salt and spices until well blended. Stir in the cubes of lamb and leave to marinate at room temperature for at least 4 hours.

Halve and stone the apricots. Cut the onions in half lengthways and cut each half into quarters. Drain the lamb and put alternate pieces of lamb, apricot and onion on to eight kebab skewers. Grill the kebabs under a high heat, turning them frequently, for about 12 minutes or until the cubes of lamb are browned on all sides.

Serves 4

Tamari beef parcels

4 thin lean slices of quick-fry steak
1 green pepper, seeded and thinly sliced
1 medium onion, skinned and thinly sliced
4 tomatoes, skinned and thinly sliced
1 carrot, trimmed, scrubbed and grated
freshly ground sea salt and pepper
30 ml (2 tbsp) tamari sauce

Cut four 30.5-cm (12-inch) squares of foil and place one steak on each. Arrange the vegetables on top of the meat in layers, season well with salt and pepper and spoon over the tamari sauce. Fold the foil over and seal to enclose the meat and vegetables. Place on a baking sheet and cook in the oven at 190°C (375°F) mark 5 for 25–30 minutes until the meat and vegetables are tender.

Serves 4

Lemon tarragon escalopes

45 ml (3 level tbsp) plain wholemeal flour
freshly ground sea salt and pepper
8 thin pork fillet escalopes
175 g (6 oz) fresh wholemeal breadcrumbs
60 ml (4 level tbsp) chopped fresh parsley
15 ml (1 level tbsp) chopped fresh tarragon
1 garlic clove, skinned and crushed
grated rind and juice of 1 lemon
2 eggs, beaten
50 g (2 oz) butter
30 ml (2 tbsp) sunflower oil
lemon slices and watercress to garnish

Season the flour with salt and pepper and toss the escalopes in the flour. Mix together the breadcrumbs, herbs, garlic and lemon rind. Dip the escalopes in the egg and coat in the crumb mixture.

Melt the butter in a large frying pan with the oil and lemon juice. Add four of the escalopes and cook for 2 minutes on each side, until crisp and golden. Transfer to a warm serving dish and cook the remaining escalopes. Place on the serving dish and garnish with the lemon slices and watercress.

Serves 4

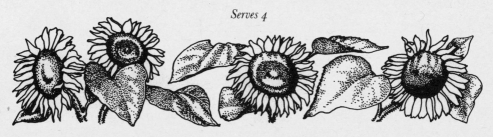

Shoulder of lamb stuffed with apricots

half a shoulder of lamb, boned and trimmed of fat
300 ml ($\frac{1}{2}$ pint) chicken stock
2 apricots
15 ml (1 level tbsp) chopped fresh mint
30 ml (2 tbsp) natural yogurt

For the stuffing
50 g (2 oz) fresh wholemeal breadcrumbs
30 ml (2 tbsp) natural yogurt
1 garlic clove, skinned and crushed
freshly ground sea salt and pepper
a little freshly grated nutmeg
2 apricots
15 ml (1 level tbsp) chopped fresh mint
15 ml (1 level tbsp) chopped fresh thyme

To make the stuffing, mix the breadcrumbs, yogurt, garlic, seasoning and nutmeg and leave for 15 minutes.

Stone and finely chop the apricots and mix them into the breadcrumb mixture with the chopped mint and thyme. Spread the cut surface of the meat with the breadcrumb mixture. Re-shape the meat and tie with strong thread. Set the meat on a rack in a roasting tin and roast at 180°C (350°F) mark 4 for $1\frac{1}{2}$ hours, until tender.

Take the lamb from the tin and put it on a warm carving dish. Pour away any fat and put the pan on top of the cooker. Pour in the stock and bring to the boil, stirring in any residue from the bottom of the pan. Stone and finely chop the apricots and mix into the stock with the mint. Leave to simmer gently while carving the lamb. Take the pan from the heat and mix the yogurt into the sauce. To serve, arrange the stuffed lamb slices on a warm serving dish and pour the apricot sauce over the top.

Serves 4

Hazelnut topped fish

700 g ($1\frac{1}{2}$ lb) haddock fillets
freshly ground sea salt and pepper
pinch of nutmeg
30 ml (2 level tbsp) chopped fresh parsley
30 ml (2 tbsp) milk
25 g (1 oz) hazelnuts, chopped and toasted
75 g (3 oz) Cheddar cheese, grated
75 g (3 oz) fresh wholemeal breadcrumbs

Cut the fish into slices and arrange in a greased baking dish. Season with salt, pepper and nutmeg and add the parsley and milk. Mix the nuts, cheese and breadcrumbs and sprinkle over the fish. Bake at 180°C (350°F) mark 4 for 30 minutes, until crisp.

Serves 4

Marinated chicken with peanut sauce

60 ml (4 tbsp) olive oil
30 ml (2 tbsp) herb vinegar
10 ml (2 level tsp) Dijon mustard
grated rind and juice of $\frac{1}{2}$ a lemon
15 ml (1 tbsp) tamari sauce
1 garlic clove, skinned and crushed
freshly ground sea salt and pepper
4 chicken portions, skinned
tomato wedges and watercress sprigs to garnish

For the sauce
1 small onion, skinned and chopped
2 large tomatoes, skinned and chopped
1 garlic clove, skinned and chopped
15 ml (1 level tbsp) tomato purée
75 ml (3 fl oz) chicken stock
15 ml (1 tbsp) tamari sauce
60 ml (4 level tbsp) peanut butter

Whisk together the oil, vinegar, mustard, lemon rind and juice, tamari sauce, garlic and seasoning until well blended. Place the chicken in a shallow dish, pour over the marinade, cover and leave for 2 hours.

Transfer the chicken and marinade to the base of a grill pan and grill under a medium heat for 30–40 minutes, basting frequently, until tender and golden brown.

To make the sauce, blend all the ingredients together in a blender until smooth. Pour into a saucepan and heat gently for 10 minutes.

Arrange the chicken portions on a warm serving dish. Pour over any remaining juices and garnish with tomato and watercress. Serve the peanut sauce separately.

Serves 4

Goulash

700 g (1½ lb) lean stewing steak
1 large onion, skinned and chopped
1 green pepper, seeded and chopped
2 large tomatoes, skinned and chopped
10 ml (2 level tsp) paprika
45 ml (3 level tbsp) tomato purée
pinch of grated nutmeg
freshly ground sea salt and pepper
1 bouquet garni
300 ml (½ pint) beef stock
150 ml (¼ pint) beer
150 ml (¼ pint) natural yogurt
chopped fresh parsley to garnish

Cut the meat into 2.5-cm (1-inch) cubes and place with the vegetables in a flameproof casserole. Add the paprika, tomato purée, nutmeg, seasoning and bouquet garni. Pour the stock and beer into a pan, bring to the boil and pour into the casserole. Cover and cook in the oven at 170°C (325°F) mark 3 for 1½–2 hours until tender. Remove the bouquet garni. Spoon the yogurt over the top and sprinkle with parsley.

Serves 6

Bean and aubergine curry

225 g (8 oz) black-eye beans, soaked (see page 23)
225 g (8 oz) aubergine
freshly ground sea salt and pepper
25 g (1 oz) butter
1 large onion, skinned and sliced
2.5 ml (½ level tsp) ground ginger
2.5 ml (½ level tsp) ground turmeric
2.5 ml (½ level tsp) ground coriander
30 ml (2 level tbsp) curry paste
15 ml (1 level tbsp) plain wholemeal flour
300 ml (½ pint) chicken stock or water

Drain the beans and cook in boiling water for about 50 minutes until almost tender, then drain again. Trim and slice the aubergine, spread the slices out on a plate and sprinkle with salt. Leave to stand for 30 minutes, then wash in cold water and dry thoroughly.

Heat the butter in a saucepan and sauté the onion for about 5 minutes until soft. Add the spices and curry paste. Cook gently, stirring, for a further 5 minutes. Stir in the flour, then gradually add the stock. Bring to the boil, then add the beans and aubergine slices. Cover and simmer very gently for 30 minutes until the aubergine is tender. Adjust the seasoning and serve with brown rice.

Serves 4

Marinated pheasant casserole

1 large oven-ready cock pheasant
15 g ($\frac{1}{2}$ oz) butter
1 small onion, skinned and finely chopped
1 small carrot, trimmed, scrubbed and finely chopped
1 small stick of celery, trimmed, washed and finely chopped
150 ml ($\frac{1}{4}$ pint) stock made with the pheasant giblets
bouquet garni

For the marinade
150 ml ($\frac{1}{4}$ pint) dry red wine
15 ml (1 tbsp) olive oil
1 carrot, trimmed, scrubbed and roughly chopped
1 medium onion, skinned and roughly chopped
1 stick of celery, trimmed, washed and roughly chopped
bouquet garni
5 ml (1 level tsp) black peppercorns

Truss the pheasant. Put all the ingredients for the marinade into a large saucepan and bring to the boil. Leave until cold. Turn the pheasant in the marinade, cover and leave at room temperature for about 8 hours, turning and basting from time to time.

Take out the pheasant and strain and reserve the marinade. Melt the butter in a large, flameproof casserole, add the pheasant and cook to brown all over. Remove the pheasant from the pan and stir in the onion, carrot and celery. Cover and cook gently for about 5 minutes until soft. Put the pheasant on top of the vegetables, pour in the stock and the reserved marinade and bring to the boil. Add the bouquet garni, cover and cook in the oven at 180°C (350°F) mark 4 for 1$\frac{1}{2}$ hours until the pheasant is tender. Remove the pheasant from the casserole and joint it. Put the pieces into a heated serving dish and spoon over all the juices and vegetables from the casserole.

Serves 4

Sauté chicken with carrot

Illustrated in colour opposite

6 chicken breast portions
700 g (1½ lb) carrots, trimmed and scrubbed
50 g (2 oz) butter or vegetable margarine
2 medium onions, skinned and sliced
2 oranges
15 ml (1 level tbsp) demerara sugar
45 ml (3 level tbsp) chopped fresh parsley
400 ml (¾ pint) chicken stock
freshly ground sea salt and pepper
60 ml (4 tbsp) natural yogurt
chopped fresh parsley to garnish

Remove the skin, fat and bone from the meat and cut the flesh into large chunks. Cut the carrots into 7.5 × 0.5-cm (3 × ¼-inch) strips. Melt the fat in a large saucepan and fry the chicken pieces until golden brown. Remove from the pan. Add the onion and sauté for about 10 minutes until well browned. Add the grated rind of the oranges, the carrots, sugar and parsley. Replace the chicken and pour over the stock and season well. Bring to the boil, cover and simmer for about 30 minutes until the chicken is tender.

Remove the pith from the oranges and separate the oranges into segments. Remove the pan from the heat and stir in the orange segments with the yogurt. Serve garnished with chopped parsley and accompanied by plain boiled brown rice.

Serves 6

Roast pheasant

2 large bunches of fresh parsley, thyme and marjoram
1 brace of young oven-ready pheasants
40 g (1½ oz) butter or 4 rashers of unsmoked streaky bacon
30 ml (2 level tbsp) plain wholemeal flour
300 ml (½ pint) stock made with the pheasant giblets

Place a bunch of herbs inside each pheasant, truss the pheasants and put them on a rack in a roasting tin. Either spread the breasts well with butter or lay two rashers of bacon over each bird. Cover completely with foil and roast in the oven at 200°C (400°F) mark 6 for 45 minutes. Remove the foil and bacon rashers and cook for a further 5 minutes. Baste the birds, dredge with flour and cook for 5 minutes more until crisp and golden.

Transfer the pheasants to a warmed serving dish and, if you plucked them yourself, decorate them with tail feathers. Carve them at the table.

To make the gravy, pour all the fat out of the roasting tin and place the tin on top of the cooker. Pour in the stock and bring to the boil, scraping in any residue from the bottom of the pan. Simmer the gravy for 2 minutes and serve in a warm sauce boat.

Serves 6–8

NOTE Another delicious accompaniment for pheasant is Wholemeal bread sauce (see page 185).

Seafood curry

Illustrated in colour opposite

450 g (1 lb) fresh haddock fillet
1 fresh green chilli
45 ml (3 tbsp) sunflower oil
1 large onion, skinned and sliced
25 g (1 oz) desiccated coconut
15 ml (1 level tbsp) plain wholemeal flour
5 ml (1 level tsp) ground coriander
150 ml ($\frac{1}{4}$ pint) white wine
25 g (1 oz) peanuts, toasted
100 g (4 oz) peeled prawns
freshly ground sea salt and pepper
chopped fresh parsley and toasted coconut to garnish

Skin the haddock and cut into 2.5-cm (1-inch) chunks. Halve the chilli, remove the seeds and finely chop the flesh. Heat the oil in a large frying pan and fry the onion for about 10 minutes, until browned.

Mix together the coconut, flour and coriander and toss with the haddock and chopped chilli. Add to the pan and fry gently until golden, stirring occasionally. Pour in the wine, bring to the boil and add the peanuts, prawns and seasoning. Cover and simmer for 5–10 minutes, or until the fish is tender. Adjust the seasoning and garnish with parsley and coconut. Serve with brown rice.

Serves 4

Orange marinated mullet

30 ml (2 tbsp) sunflower oil
60 ml (4 tbsp) rosemary vinegar
freshly ground sea salt and pepper
1 medium onion, skinned and finely chopped
2 oranges
4 medium red mullet, cleaned and heads removed
watercress to garnish

Whisk together the oil, vinegar and seasoning and add the onion. Cut four slices from one of the oranges and reserve for garnish. Add the grated rind and juice of the remaining oranges to the marinade. Cut three slashes on each side of the mullet and place in a shallow dish. Pour over the marinade and leave, covered, for 30 minutes, turning once.

Place the fish in the bottom of a grill pan and pour over the marinade. Grill under a medium heat for 15–20 minutes, turning once and basting frequently, until tender. Transfer to a warm serving dish and pour over any remaining marinade. Garnish with the reserved orange slices and watercress.

Serves 4

Vegetable couscous

450 g (1 lb) couscous
400 ml ($\frac{3}{4}$ pint) tepid water
4 courgettes, washed and trimmed
1 red pepper, seeded
1 green pepper, seeded
2 medium onions, skinned
2 carrots, trimmed and scrubbed
225 g (8 oz) turnips, peeled
1 small cauliflower, trimmed and washed
4 large tomatoes, skinned
2 garlic cloves, skinned and crushed
1.1 litres (2 pints) vegetable stock
freshly ground sea salt and pepper
225 g (8 oz) chick peas, soaked (see page 23)
25 g (1 oz) blanched almonds
5 ml (1 level tsp) turmeric
10 ml (2 level tsp) paprika
2.5 ml ($\frac{1}{2}$ level tsp) coriander
75 g (3 oz) butter
100 g (4 oz) dried apricots, soaked overnight

Place the couscous in a large bowl with the water and leave to soak for 1 hour. Meanwhile, cut the courgettes into 1-cm ($\frac{1}{2}$-inch) slices and roughly dice the peppers, onions, carrots and turnips. Cut the cauliflower into small florets and chop the tomatoes. Place the vegetables in a large saucepan with the garlic, stock, seasoning, chick peas, nuts and spices. Bring to the boil, cover and simmer for 30 minutes.

Drain the couscous grains and place them in a steamer on the saucepan over the vegetables. Cover and continue cooking for a further 40 minutes, then remove the steamer and cover the saucepan.

Place the couscous in a large mixing bowl. Melt the butter and beat it into the couscous with 50 ml (2 fl oz) salt water. Leave for 15 minutes. Drain and quarter the apricots, add them to the vegetables and simmer for 15 minutes. Stir the couscous well to remove any lumps and return it to the steamer over the simmering vegetables for 20 minutes, covered. Serve the vegetables and couscous separately in warm serving dishes.

Serves 6

Cod and cucumber mornay

4 large cod cutlets
freshly ground sea salt and pepper
10 ml (2 level tsp) chopped fresh parsley
150 ml ($\frac{1}{4}$ pint) dry cider
$\frac{1}{2}$ a cucumber, peeled and diced
150 ml ($\frac{1}{4}$ pint) milk
100 g (4 oz) Cheddar cheese, grated

Place the fish in an ovenproof dish or casserole, season with salt and pepper, add the parsley and pour over the cider. Cover and bake in the oven at 180°C (350°F) mark 4 for about 20 minutes, or until the fish is cooked and slightly flaky.

While the fish is cooking, put the cucumber in a pan with the milk, then season to taste and simmer gently for 10 minutes. When the fish is cooked, pour over the cucumber mixture and sprinkle with the grated cheese. Grill until the cheese melts and turns golden brown.

Serves 4

Persian lamb

225 g (8 oz) dried apricots
300 ml ($\frac{1}{2}$ pint) boiling water
2.3-kg (5-lb) leg of lamb, boned and trimmed of fat
15 ml (1 tbsp) vegetable oil
1 large onion, skinned and chopped
5 ml (1 level tsp) ground coriander
2.5 ml ($\frac{1}{2}$ level tsp) ground cinnamon
5 ml (1 level tsp) ground cumin
freshly ground sea salt and pepper
350 g (12 oz) brown rice, cooked

Place the apricots in a bowl, cover with the water and leave to soak for 2 hours. Cut the meat into 2.5-cm (1-inch) cubes.

Drain the apricots, reserving the liquid. Heat the oil in a large saucepan. Add the lamb and onion and cook for 10 minutes, stirring, until lightly browned. Add the spices, seasoning and the liquid in which the apricots were soaked. Cut the apricots in half and stir them into the lamb. Cover and simmer gently for $1\frac{1}{2}$ hours, or until the lamb is tender, stirring occasionally.

Meanwhile, bring a pan of lightly salted water to the boil. Stir in the rice, cover and simmer for 40–45 minutes or until the rice is just tender. Drain well. To serve, spoon the rice around the edge of a warm serving dish and pour the lamb into the centre.

Serves 4

Pork fillet with cider

450 g (1 lb) pork fillet, trimmed of fat
25 g (1 oz) butter
1 medium onion, skinned and chopped
2 large eating apples, cored and chopped
175 g (6 oz) brown rice
15 ml (1 level tbsp) chopped fresh tarragon
400 ml ($\frac{3}{4}$ pint) dry cider
150 ml ($\frac{1}{4}$ pint) vegetable stock
30 ml (2 level tbsp) French mustard
freshly ground sea salt and pepper
50 g (2 oz) mixed nuts, roughly chopped
25 g (1 oz) seedless raisins
chopped fresh parsley to garnish

Cut the meat diagonally into 1-cm ($\frac{1}{2}$-inch) slices. Melt the butter in a flameproof casserole and brown the pork on both sides. Remove the meat from the dish, add the onion and apple and sauté in the residual butter for 5 minutes until soft. Stir in the rice, tarragon, cider, stock, mustard and seasoning. Bring to the boil, then remove from the heat and stir in the nuts and raisins.

Arrange the pork, overlapping, on top of the rice. Cover the dish tightly and bake in the oven at 170°C (325°F) mark 3 for 1 hour or until tender. Sprinkle over the parsley.

Serves 4

Grilled sole and grapes

700 g ($1\frac{1}{2}$ lb) lemon sole fillets
olive oil
freshly ground sea salt and pepper
1 lemon, quartered
a few grapes and parsley sprigs to garnish

Line a grill pan with foil. Brush the sole fillets very lightly with oil and sprinkle with salt and pepper. Arrange the fillets in the grill pan and grill under a medium heat for about 5 minutes on each side, or until the fish is cooked and slightly flaky.

Just before serving, squeeze a lemon wedge over each fillet and garnish with grapes and parsley sprigs.

Serves 4

Crumbly-topped Spanish pork

1.6-kg (3½-lb) lean loin of pork, boned and skinned
1 large garlic clove, skinned
freshly ground sea salt and pepper
1 small onion, skinned and chopped
1 stick of celery, trimmed, washed and chopped
75 g (3 oz) blanched almonds, roughly chopped
100 g (4 oz) fresh wholemeal breadcrumbs
1 egg, beaten
watercress to garnish

Lay the pork out flat and make small cuts in it. Cut the garlic into thin slivers and insert the slivers in the pork. Season well.

Place the onion and celery in a small bowl with the nuts and breadcrumbs and season. Bind together with the egg. Spread this mixture over the top of the pork to cover the meat. Place in a roasting tin and roast in the oven at 190°C (375°F) mark 5 for 2 hours until tender. Transfer to a warm serving dish and garnish with watercress.

Serves 6

Pigeons braised with red cabbage

4 small thyme sprigs
4 small parsley sprigs
4 oven-ready pigeons
25 g (1 oz) butter
1 large onion, skinned and thinly sliced
1 small red cabbage, trimmed and shredded
90 ml (6 tbsp) dry red wine
grated rind and juice of 1 large orange
15 ml (1 tbsp) red wine vinegar
15 ml (1 level tbsp) chopped capers
pinch of cayenne pepper
1 large orange, to garnish

Put a sprig of thyme and parsley inside each pigeon and truss them. Melt the butter in a large flameproof casserole, add the pigeons and cook until browned. Remove from the casserole, add the onion and cook for about 5 minutes until soft. Stir in the cabbage, then pour in the red wine and the orange juice and bring to the boil. Add the orange rind, vinegar, chopped capers and cayenne pepper. Remove from the heat and place the pigeons in the casserole. Cover and bake in the oven at 180°C (350°F) mark 4 for 1½ hours until the pigeons are tender.

When the pigeons are cooked, arrange them on a serving dish surrounded by the cabbage and onion. Cut the orange into thin slices, form them into twists and use to garnish the dish.

Serves 4

Salads and Vegetables

Instead of being neglected, as in so many styles of cooking, vegetables often take pride of place in the wholefood kitchen. There are so many to choose from right through the year. You can cook them in countless different ways, serve them raw in fresh, crunchy salads and even make them the basis of main dishes.

Always make sure that you buy the freshest and best vegetables you can find, and when you get home store them carefully in a cool dry place in order to keep them in the best condition until you want to use them. But never keep them for too long, as their goodness starts to diminish as soon as they are picked.

When you are preparing vegetables, whether for salads or for cooking, the less they are handled the more goodness they will retain. Radish roses and celery cut and soaked to look like crackers are all very attractive, but a whole radish and an uncut stick of celery contain more goodness. A large percentage of the goodness in many vegetables lies just under the surface, so only peel them when it is absolutely necessary. Give root vegetables a good scrub and wash cabbages and leafy vegetables quickly. Never leave vegetables soaking in water as this dissolves away the water-soluble vitamins B and C. When you must chop or slice vegetables, always make sure that your knife is as sharp as possible since a blunt knife will flatten the plant cells rather than cut them cleanly, so causing yet more vitamin loss.

Salads

A salad ought to feature at least once a day in a wholefood diet. A salad isn't just a limp lettuce leaf garnished with a bottle of salad cream; they can be exciting and imaginative and very varied. Nearly every vegetable can be served raw, even ones like turnips and swedes which are most often associated with winter stews.

To make salads interesting, combine two or more vegetables but make sure their textures and flavours match. Fruits can be added to salads most effectively. The light, summer ones go with more delicate vegetables like lettuce and cucumber; and crunchy apples and refreshing oranges go best in winter mixtures of celery, cabbage or grated roots. Dried fruits provide touches of colour and flavour, and extra goodness can be added by way of chopped nuts or the small seeds like sesame or poppy.

The secret of a good salad is in the dressing and if you have one basic mixture and many additions, the combinations of tastes and flavours you can produce are unending. To make a basic French dressing mix 45 ml (3 tbsp) oil with 15 ml (1 tbsp) something sharp. The most universal oil is olive, but you can replace it with sunflower or groundnut oil or, for special occasions, sesame or walnut. The sharp addition can be lemon, orange or grapefruit juice or a vinegar. Malt vinegar is too robust for most salads, although it goes well with red cabbage. Instead, use white or red wine vinegars or a cider vinegar.

15 ml (1 tbsp) of tahini (sesame) paste or tamari sauce can be added for extra flavour and richness; or you can add tomato purée or a dash of Worcestershire sauce. Chopped fresh herbs will give a whole variety of flavours, and spices such as cinnamon, curry powder or paprika can be added sparingly.

Vegetables

The easiest and simplest way of cooking vegetables is to boil them. This does not have to mean that you end up with sloppy cabbage and tasteless carrots. Boiled vegetables can be light and delicious provided you go about it in the right way. Use only as much water as will barely cover the vegetables and salt it only lightly. Bring it to the boil first and then quickly put in the vegetables. Bring the water back to the boil and lower the heat under it so it gently simmers. Cook the vegetables, covered, until they are only just tender and still slightly crisp. Drain them and serve them as soon as you can, perhaps with a knob of butter or vegetable margarine and sprinkled with chopped fresh herbs.

Steaming is a very popular method with wholefood cooks since no fat is used and the vegetables do not actually come into contact with the water, so retaining most of their

water-soluble vitamins. It takes about half as long again as boiling, but preserves a better flavour. You need a perforated vegetable steamer or a large colander which you can cover with a saucepan lid or with foil. Prepare the vegetables and put them into the steamer. Bring some water to the boil in a saucepan (not too much as it must not bubble up through the holes of the steamer), lower in the steamer with its vegetables, put on the lid or foil, turn down the heat so the water is just simmering and cook the vegetables until they are only just tender. If they are piled in the steamer in more than one layer, turn them over once to ensure even cooking.

Simmering and braising are two methods of cooking which can make vegetables into a richer and more interesting side dish. Both methods start in the same way: heat a little butter, oil or vegetable margarine in a casserole or saucepan, add a skinned and chopped onion, if liked, and cook gently until soft. Then stir in the prepared vegetables, pour in a little liquid (see below), cover, and either put into the oven or let the vegetables simmer gently on top of the cooker until tender. The oven method will take slightly longer. You can flavour braised and simmered vegetables with chopped herbs or with spices such as paprika, nutmeg or caraway. Water can be used as the cooking liquid or you can replace it with stock, wine, beer or cider; and for an even richer dish you could flavour the liquid with tomato purée, tamari sauce or Worcestershire sauce.

Root vegetables can be cut into chunks and baked in the oven, either in a little butter or oil or in about 1 cm ($\frac{1}{2}$ inch) stock. Whole, skinned onions are delicious baked in stock and, after cooking, they can be sprinkled with herbs or with grated cheese. Sliced or diced root vegetables can also be baked in parcels of lightly greased foil.

Stir-frying and stir-braising are two Chinese cooking methods which are rapidly becoming popular in this country. They are both very quick methods and so preserve much of the vegetables' goodness. They are suitable for either individual vegetables or mixtures and the vegetables must be chopped or sliced quite thinly. To stir-fry, heat 60 ml (4 tbsp) oil per 450 g (1 lb) vegetables in a large frying pan or Chinese wok on a high heat. For flavour, you could add a skinned and chopped garlic clove as the oil heats. Put in the prepared vegetables and stir them around on the heat for about 2 minutes or until they just begin to soften. Then pour in about 90 ml (6 tbsp) liquid – usually stock or sherry or a mixture – with 15 ml (1 tbsp) tamari sauce and boil rapidly until reduced by half. The vegetables are then ready to serve. You can make a hot salad-type dish by adding 30 ml (2 tbsp) wine vinegar instead of the liquid.

Stir-braising is mostly used for the crunchier vegetables like cauliflower or celery, or for the tougher ones like curly kale. After stirring them around on the heat in the same way as for stir-frying, add 150 ml ($\frac{1}{4}$ pint) liquid per 450 g (1 lb) vegetables. Cover the pan and leave the vegetables to cook gently for about 10 minutes.

Potatoes are the favourite filler vegetable in this country and, like root vegetables, most of their goodness is just under the skin. It is best, therefore, to peel them as rarely as possible. The most nutritious way of cooking old potatoes is to bake them in their jackets either in the oven or in a special earthenware potato pot. If you want crispy roast potatoes, simply scrub them, cut them up and roast them in hot butter (see page 154). They will not only be more nutritious than potatoes that have been first par-boiled and peeled, but they will also have a far better flavour. If creamed potatoes are most suited to your main meal, boil them in their skins first, peel them while they are still hot and mash them with yogurt instead of cream. New baby potatoes are best boiled in their skins and served quite plainly or tossed with butter, mint or parsley. You can also slice them and steam them with a sprig of mint.

With all these delicious ways of cooking vegetables, the wholefood cook can make full use of them as tasty nutritious dishes in their own right. They need no longer be treated solely as an accompaniment to other things.

Salade aux noix
1 small Iceberg lettuce
50 g (2 oz) walnut halves

For the dressing
90 ml (6 tbsp) walnut or olive oil
15 ml (1 tbsp) white wine vinegar
15 ml (1 tbsp) lemon juice
pinch of mustard powder
pinch of demerara sugar
freshly ground sea salt and pepper

Wash and finely shred the lettuce and break the walnuts into small pieces. Place the lettuce and walnuts in a salad bowl. Whisk all the dressing ingredients together until well blended or put them in a screw-topped jar and shake vigorously. Just before serving, pour this dressing over the salad and toss well together.

Serves 4

Potato layer

90 ml (6 tbsp) soured cream
45 ml (3 level tbsp) chopped fresh parsley
1 garlic clove, skinned and crushed
1 medium onion, skinned and finely chopped
freshly ground sea salt and pepper
700 g (1½ lb) even-sized potatoes, peeled
chopped fresh parsley to garnish

Grease and line the base of an 18-cm (7-inch) diameter cake tin. Mix the soured cream, chopped parsley, garlic, onion and seasoning. Thinly slice the potatoes and arrange in the tin in overlapping layers. Pour the soured cream and onion dressing over each layer, finishing with a layer of potato. Cover with foil and press down well. Bake in the oven at 190°C (375°F) mark 5 for about 1 hour. Turn out and sprinkle with chopped fresh parsley. Serve with cold lean meats.

Serves 4

Mushroom salad

This is an ideal accompaniment to fish.

100 g (4 oz) flat mushrooms, wiped
45 ml (3 tbsp) olive oil
15 ml (1 tbsp) lemon juice or cider vinegar
15 ml (1 level tbsp) chopped fresh parsley
freshly ground sea salt and pepper

Remove the mushroom stalks. (Use them, if liked, in a stew or sauce.) Slice the mushrooms very thinly into a serving dish and add the other ingredients. Leave the mushrooms to marinate in the dressing for 30 minutes before serving.

Serves 2

Winter salad

225 g (8 oz) lean unsmoked bacon, rinded
1 head of chicory
2 eating apples, cored and chopped
15 ml (1 tbsp) lemon juice
100 g (4 oz) peanuts
150 ml (¼ pint) natural yogurt
freshly ground sea salt and pepper

Grill the bacon until crisp. Leave until cold then roughly chop. Trim and cut the chicory into rings, then wash well. Toss the apple pieces in the lemon juice. Place all the ingredients in a salad bowl and mix well together.

Serves 4

Brussels sprouts and chestnuts

This mixture makes a good accompaniment to Christmas poultry.

225 g (8 oz) chestnuts
300 ml ($\frac{1}{2}$ pint) vegetable stock
1 stick of celery, trimmed and washed
5 ml (1 level tsp) Barbados sugar
450 g (1 lb) Brussels sprouts, trimmed
freshly ground sea salt and pepper

Put the chestnuts into a saucepan of cold water and bring to the boil. Remove from the heat, drain and leave to cool. When they are cool enough to handle, remove both the outer and inner skins. Put the nuts in a saucepan, cover with the stock and add the celery and sugar. Bring to the boil. Reduce the heat, cover and simmer gently for 35–40 minutes, or until the chestnuts are soft.

Meanwhile, cook the Brussels sprouts separately in boiling salted water for 10–15 minutes, or until they are just tender. Drain the nuts and remove the celery. Drain the Brussels sprouts and mix the nuts and sprouts together. Season to taste before serving.

Serves 4

Cauliflower with sweet and sour sauce

1 large cauliflower
40 g (1$\frac{1}{2}$ oz) butter
1 medium onion, skinned and finely chopped
30 ml (2 level tbsp) demerara sugar
45 ml (3 level tbsp) tomato purée
30 ml (2 tbsp) white wine vinegar
10 ml (2 tsp) tamari sauce
60 ml (4 tbsp) white wine
freshly ground sea salt and pepper
chopped fresh parsley to garnish

Divide the cauliflower into small florets and cook in boiling salted water for about 5 minutes until just tender. Drain well, put into a heated serving dish and keep warm.

Melt the butter in a saucepan and fry the onion for 5 minutes, until soft. Stir in all the remaining ingredients, except the parsley, and cook for a further 3–4 minutes. Pour the sauce over the cauliflower and sprinkle with chopped fresh parsley to serve.

Serves 4

Spring greens with Worcestershire sauce

25 g (1 oz) butter or vegetable margarine
1 medium onion, skinned and thinly sliced
450 g (1 lb) spring greens, washed and finely chopped
150 ml ($\frac{1}{4}$ pint) chicken stock
15 ml (1 tbsp) Worcestershire sauce
4 tomatoes, skinned and roughly chopped

Melt the fat in a large frying pan, stir in the onion and cook for about 5 minutes until soft. Raise the heat, add the greens and cook, stirring, for 2 minutes. The pan will be piled high at first but the greens will soon sink down. Pour in the stock and Worcestershire sauce. Cover the pan and cook on a medium heat for 10 minutes until the spring greens are tender. Mix in the chopped tomatoes, cover again and cook for a further 2 minutes.

Serves 4

Baby potato and yogurt salad

700 g (1$\frac{1}{2}$ lb) tiny new potatoes, scrubbed

For the dressing
150 ml ($\frac{1}{4}$ pint) natural yogurt
15 ml (1 tbsp) olive oil
1.25 ml ($\frac{1}{4}$ level tsp) ground cumin
1.25 ml ($\frac{1}{4}$ level tsp) ground coriander
15 ml (1 level tbsp) poppy seeds

Cook the potatoes in their skins in boiling salted water for 10–15 minutes, until they are just tender. Meanwhile, make the dressing by whisking the ingredients together until well blended. Alternatively, put the dressing ingredients in a screw-topped jar and shake vigorously. Drain the potatoes and stir them immediately into the dressing. Turn into a serving dish and leave until cold before serving.

Serves 4

Unpeeled roast potatoes

900 g (2 lb) small or medium old potatoes
50 g (2 oz) butter

Scrub the potatoes and cut them into 2.5-cm (1-inch) cubes. Place the butter in a large, shallow roasting tin and put in the oven at 220°C (425°F) mark 7 until the butter is melted and really hot. Mix the potatoes into the butter and bake in the oven for 1 hour, stirring occasionally, until they are really crisp and golden brown.

Serves 4

Spinach sauté with peanuts

450 g (1 lb) spinach, trimmed and chopped
25 g (1 oz) butter or vegetable margarine
1 medium onion, skinned and chopped
50 g (2 oz) peanuts, chopped
freshly ground sea salt and pepper

Wash the spinach and put the wet leaves into a large pan. Cover and cook gently, turning the spinach over occasionally, for 10–12 minutes, or until it is tender. Drain, chop roughly and keep hot.

Melt the fat in a pan, add the onions and cook for 5–10 minutes, or until lightly browned. Add the peanuts and cook for 2 minutes. Stir in the cooked spinach and season to taste. Heat through and serve immediately.

Serves 2

Celeriac rémoulade

1 large head of celeriac
30 ml (2 tbsp) lemon juice
300 ml ($\frac{1}{2}$ pint) mayonnaise (see page 171)
freshly ground sea salt and pepper
30 ml (2 level tbsp) chopped fresh chives
30 ml (2 level tbsp) French mustard
1 lettuce, washed
chopped fresh parsley to garnish

Peel and coarsely grate the celeriac and toss in the lemon juice to prevent discoloration. Add the remaining ingredients, except the lettuce and parsley, and mix well together. Serve on a bed of lettuce, sprinkled with chopped parsley.

Serves 6

Braised turnips with horseradish

450 g (1 lb) turnips, peeled
25 g (1 oz) butter or vegetable margarine
150 ml ($\frac{1}{4}$ pint) chicken stock
15 ml (1 level tbsp) grated horseradish
15 ml (1 level tbsp) tomato purée

Cut the turnips into 1.5-cm ($\frac{3}{4}$-inch) dice. Melt the fat in a flameproof casserole, stir in the turnips and cook for about 10 minutes until just beginning to brown. Pour in the stock and bring to the boil, then stir in the horseradish and tomato purée. Cover and bake in the oven at 190°C (375°F) mark 5 for 30 minutes until the turnip is tender.

Serves 4

Celery amandine

50 g (2 oz) butter
1 small head of celery, trimmed, washed and cut diagonally into 2-cm ($\frac{3}{4}$-inch) pieces
freshly ground sea salt and pepper
7.5 ml ($1\frac{1}{2}$ level tsp) finely chopped onion
75 g (3 oz) flaked almonds
1 garlic clove, skinned and finely chopped
30 ml (2 tbsp) dry white wine

Melt half the butter in a large saucepan. Add the celery, salt and pepper, cover and cook over a low heat for 8 minutes or until the celery is tender but still crisp. Add the onion, cover and cook for 1 minute. Drain well, put the onion and celery in a heated serving dish and keep warm.

Clean out the pan and cook the almonds in the remaining butter for 2–3 minutes, stirring continuously, until brown. Add the garlic and wine and cook for a further 3 minutes. Spoon the almond mixture evenly over the celery and onion and serve hot as a vegetable accompaniment.

Serves 4

Bean and tomato salad

450 g (1 lb) French beans, trimmed
450 g (1 lb) tomatoes, sliced
15 ml (1 level tbsp) chopped fresh parsley
150 ml ($\frac{1}{4}$ pint) soured cream
freshly ground sea salt and pepper

Cook the beans in boiling salted water for 10 minutes until just tender. Drain and rinse under cold water. Place the beans and tomatoes in a serving dish. Mix the parsley, soured cream and seasoning together and pour over the salad to serve.

Serves 6

Parsnips baked in foil

4 medium parsnips, peeled
2 sage leaves, chopped
15 ml (1 level tbsp) chopped fresh parsley
50 g (2 oz) curd cheese

Lightly oil a large sheet of foil and place on a baking sheet. Cut each parsnip in half lengthways and scoop out the woody cores. Blend the chopped herbs into the cheese and use to fill the holes left by the cores. Lay the parsnips in a single layer on top of the foil and wrap them securely. Bake in the oven at 190°C (375°F) mark 5 for about $1\frac{1}{4}$ hours until the parsnips are tender.

Serves 4

Tossed fresh spinach salad

Illustrated in colour on page 178

60 ml (4 tbsp) sunflower oil
30 ml (2 tbsp) white wine vinegar
7.5 ml (1½ level tsp) chopped fresh basil
10 ml (2 level tsp) finely grated lemon rind
100 g (4 oz) spinach
1 lettuce heart
6 radishes, trimmed and sliced
6 spring onions, trimmed and sliced

Put the oil and vinegar in a screw-topped jar with the basil and lemon rind. Shake well and leave to stand.

Wash the spinach thoroughly, discarding any tough stems, then dry thoroughly. Wash and dry the lettuce. Shred the spinach and lettuce into bite-size pieces. Mix these with the sliced radishes and spring onions, pour over the dressing and toss well. Pile into a serving dish and serve as a side salad with grills or cold lean meats.

Serves 4

Celeriac and potato whirls

1.4 kg (3 lb) celeriac
30 ml (2 tbsp) lemon juice
2 large potatoes, peeled and quartered
50 g (2 oz) butter
1 egg, beaten
freshly ground sea salt and pepper
fresh parsley sprigs to garnish

Peel and quarter the celeriac and put the pieces in a bowl of cold water with the lemon juice to prevent discoloration. Drain the celeriac and cook with the potatoes in a saucepan of boiling salted water for 20–30 minutes, or until tender. Drain, then sieve or mash the vegetables. Add the butter, egg and seasoning and beat until smooth. Leave to cool slightly, then fill a piping bag fitted with a large star nozzle and pipe the mixture in rosettes on to a greased baking sheet. Bake in the oven at 200°C (400°F) mark 6 for 25–35 minutes until golden brown. Serve garnished with parsley sprigs.

Serves 4

Almond, apricot and alfalfa salad

225 g (8 oz) almonds
100 g (4 oz) dried apricots
10 ml (2 level tsp) curry powder
10 ml (2 level tsp) ground cumin
90 ml (6 tbsp) olive oil
grated rind and juice of 1 lemon
1 garlic clove, skinned and crushed
freshly ground sea salt
100 g (4 oz) sprouted alfalfa

Blanch the almonds in boiling water, then squeeze them out of their skins. Cut the apricots into quarters. Put the curry powder and cumin into a bowl and gradually beat in the oil, lemon rind and juice, garlic and salt. Stir in the almonds and apricots and leave to stand for 15 minutes until the flavour of the dressing has been absorbed.

Divide the alfalfa between four serving plates, arrange the almonds and apricots on top and pour over the dressing.

Serves 4

Lemon Jerusalem artichokes

700 g ($1\frac{1}{2}$ lb) Jerusalem artichokes
1 slice of lemon
25 g (1 oz) butter or vegetable margarine
4 spring onions, trimmed, washed and finely sliced
25 g (1 oz) fresh granary breadcrumbs
freshly ground sea salt and pepper
25 g (1 oz) walnuts, roughly chopped
grated rind and juice of $\frac{1}{2}$ a lemon
150 ml ($\frac{1}{4}$ pint) soured cream
lemon wedges to garnish

Wash and peel the artichokes and place them in a pan with the lemon slice. Cover with cold salted water and bring to the boil. Simmer gently, covered, for about 20 minutes, until tender.

Meanwhile, melt the fat in a saucepan and fry the spring onions for 2–3 minutes, remove from the heat and add the remaining ingredients, except the lemon wedges, stirring well. Gently reheat but do not allow to boil.

When the artichokes are cooked, drain, then slice and arrange them in a warm serving dish. Pour the sauce over the artichokes and serve garnished with lemon wedges.

Serves 4

Spicy cauliflower medley

Illustrated in colour opposite

30 ml (2 tbsp) sunflower oil
2.5 ml ($\frac{1}{2}$ level tsp) ground cumin
2.5 ml ($\frac{1}{2}$ level tsp) ground coriander
2.5 ml ($\frac{1}{2}$ level tsp) mustard powder
2.5 ml ($\frac{1}{2}$ level tsp) ground turmeric
pinch of cayenne pepper
1 large cauliflower, trimmed
225 g (8 oz) carrots, trimmed, scrubbed and sliced
1 medium onion, skinned and chopped
1 cooking apple, peeled, cored and chopped
100 ml (4 fl oz) water
300 ml ($\frac{1}{2}$ pint) natural yogurt

Heat the oil in a large pan, add the spices and cook gently for 2 minutes, stirring. Divide the cauliflower into florets and add to the pan with the carrots, onion and apple. Cook for 5 minutes, stirring, until soft. Add the water and yogurt, stir well, cover and simmer gently for about 10 minutes until the vegetables are tender.

Serves 4

Crunchy salad

Illustrated in colour on page 177

350 g (12 oz) white cabbage, trimmed
225 g (8 oz) carrots, trimmed and scrubbed
1 small onion, skinned
1 satsuma
15 g ($\frac{1}{2}$ oz) currants
5 ml (1 level tsp) grated orange rind
50 g (2 oz) red pepper, seeded and sliced

For the dressing
150 ml ($\frac{1}{4}$ pint) natural yogurt
5 ml (1 level tsp) grated orange rind
15 ml (1 tbsp) orange juice
5 ml (1 level tsp) chopped fresh mint
freshly ground sea salt and pepper

Wash and dry the cabbage thoroughly. Grate the cabbage, carrots and onion into a large bowl. Peel the satsuma and strip away all the pith. Slice and mix into the salad together with the currants and orange rind.

For the dressing, whisk all the ingredients together until well blended and pour over the salad. Scatter with the red pepper strips.

Serves 6

Quick baked potatoes

4 large potatoes, scrubbed and halved
a little sunflower oil
freshly ground sea salt

Brush the cut surfaces of the potatoes with a little oil, then sprinkle with a little salt.
Bake in the oven at 200°C (400°F) mark 6 for about 30 minutes until the tops are very
crisp and the centres soft. Brush on a little more oil during cooking, if necessary. (The
cut surface may also be scored with a knife to speed up the cooking.)

Serves 4

Bangkok salad

175 g (6 oz) mung bean sprouts, washed
1 red pepper, seeded and sliced

For the dressing
30 ml (2 tbsp) groundnut oil
15 ml (1 tbsp) white wine vinegar
5 ml (1 tsp) clear honey
5 ml (1 tsp) tamari sauce

Mix the bean sprouts and red pepper in a bowl. To make the dressing, whisk all the
ingredients together until well blended, or put them in a screw-topped jar and shake
vigorously. Pour the dressing over the bean sprouts and toss well. Leave to stand at
room temperature for 30 minutes before serving to let the flavours blend.

Serves 2

Apple and cabbage salad

2 large carrots, trimmed, scrubbed and grated
3 sticks of celery, trimmed, washed and finely chopped
175 g (6 oz) white cabbage, trimmed, washed and shredded
2 red eating apples, cored and diced
30 ml (2 tbsp) pineapple juice
30 ml (2 tbsp) sunflower oil
freshly ground sea salt and pepper
1 lettuce, washed
watercress sprigs to garnish

Combine all the vegetables and the apples in a salad bowl. Whisk the pineapple juice
and oil together until well blended and season to taste. Pour this dressing over the
vegetables and toss well. Arrange on lettuce leaves and garnish with sprigs of watercress.

Serves 4

NOTE As an alternative to pineapple juice, this salad could be tossed in a French (see page 172) or yogurt (see
page 171) dressing.

Ratatouille

Illustrated in colour on page 177

5 ml (1 tsp) olive oil
225 g (8 oz) onions, skinned and sliced
225 g (8 oz) green and gold peppers, seeded and thinly sliced
225 g (8 oz) aubergines
1 garlic clove, skinned and finely chopped
freshly ground sea salt and pepper
5 ml (1 level tsp) dried oregano
4 tomatoes, skinned and chopped
10 ml (2 tsp) white wine vinegar

Heat the oil in a wide heavy-based saucepan. Add the onions, cover the pan and cook for 5 minutes, until soft. Add the peppers, cover and continue cooking slowly for another 10 minutes until soft. Meanwhile, prepare the aubergines. Cut them into quarters lengthways. Lay the pieces on a board and cut across into 0.5-cm ($\frac{1}{4}$-inch) slices. Stir the garlic into the softened onions and peppers. Mix in the aubergine and season with the salt, pepper and oregano. Cover and simmer for 10 minutes, turning once. Add the tomatoes and vinegar, cover and cook gently for another 10 minutes until tender. Adjust the seasoning and serve hot or cold.

Serves 6

Apple, raisin and walnut salad

Illustrated in colour on page 178

30 ml (2 tbsp) lemon juice
2.5 ml ($\frac{1}{2}$ level tsp) ground cinnamon
3 crisp, green eating apples
50 g (2 oz) seedless raisins
50 g (2 oz) walnuts, roughly chopped

Mix together the lemon juice and spice. Core the apples and slice them thinly and toss the apple slices in the spiced lemon juice. Add the raisins and walnuts and toss well together. Serve as a side salad with cold lean pork, cooked bacon or chicken.

Serves 3–4

Watercress and pineapple salad

2 bunches of watercress, trimmed and washed
1 punnet of mustard and cress, washed
$\frac{1}{2}$ a small pineapple

For the dressing
60 ml (4 tbsp) olive or sunflower oil
30 ml (2 tbsp) white wine vinegar
5 ml (1 level tsp) Dijon mustard
1 garlic clove, skinned and crushed
freshly ground sea salt and pepper

Chop the watercress and put it into a salad bowl with the mustard and cress. Peel the pineapple and remove the core. Finely chop the flesh and add to the salad bowl. To make the dressing, whisk all the ingredients together until well blended, or put them in a screw-topped jar and shake vigorously. Stir into the salad.

Serves 4

Minted cucumber and celery

Illustrated in colour on page 178

$\frac{1}{2}$ a medium cucumber, finely diced
3–4 sticks of celery, trimmed, washed and finely sliced
150 ml ($\frac{1}{4}$ pint) natural yogurt
5 ml (1 level tsp) chopped fresh mint
grated rind of $\frac{1}{2}$ a lemon
freshly ground sea salt and pepper

Put the cucumber and celery into a bowl. Add the yogurt, mint, lemon rind, salt and pepper. Mix well together and chill before serving.

Serves 4

Stir-fried celery with dill

30 ml (2 tbsp) white wine vinegar
5 ml (1 level tsp) Dijon mustard
60 ml (4 tbsp) olive oil
5 ml (1 level tsp) dill seeds
1 garlic clove, skinned and finely chopped
1 small head of celery, trimmed, washed and finely chopped

Mix the vinegar and mustard together in a small bowl. Heat the oil in a large frying pan and add the dill and garlic. Cook over a high heat for 2–3 minutes until the garlic browns. Add the celery and stir for 30 seconds. Pour in the vinegar mixture and bring to the boil. Serve immediately.

Serves 4

Jerusalem artichoke and carrot purée

Illustrated in colour on page 177

450 g (1 lb) Jerusalem artichokes
10 ml (2 tsp) vinegar or lemon juice
225 g (8 oz) carrots, trimmed and scrubbed
1 medium onion, skinned
1.1 litres (2 pints) boiling water with
5 ml (1 level tsp) freshly ground sea salt added
1 bay leaf
30–45 ml (2–3 tbsp) milk
pinch of grated nutmeg
freshly ground sea salt and pepper
15 g ($\frac{1}{2}$ oz) butter
chopped fresh parsley to garnish

Wash and peel the artichokes and place them in a bowl of cold water with the vinegar or lemon juice. Halve or quarter them so that they are about the same size. Cut the carrots into small chunks. Thinly slice the onion. Drain the artichokes and slide them into the boiling salted water. Add the carrot, onion and bay leaf.

Partially cover the pan and boil for 10–15 minutes, until the vegetables are tender but firm when pricked with a fork. Drain thoroughly and remove the bay leaf. Tip the vegetables into a bowl and mash to a purée, working in the milk, nutmeg, salt and pepper to taste. Stir in the butter. If you purée the vegetables in a blender, do not add more than 45 ml (3 tbsp) milk or the final purée will be too wet.

Reheat over a medium heat, uncovered, stirring from time to time, or in the oven at 190°C (375°F) mark 5 for 15–20 minutes, until hot. Garnish with parsley.

Serves 4

Chicory salad

2 medium heads of chicory, trimmed and finely sliced
6 black olives, stoned

For the dressing
30 ml (2 tbsp) olive oil
15 ml (1 tbsp) white wine vinegar
15 ml (1 tbsp) lemon juice
5 ml (1 tsp) clear honey
1 small onion, skinned and finely grated
freshly ground sea salt and pepper

Put the chicory and olives into a bowl. To make the dressing, whisk all the ingredients together until well blended, or put them in a screw-topped jar and shake vigorously. Pour over the chicory and olives and toss well just before serving.

Serves 4

Crispy cauliflower salad

1 medium cauliflower, trimmed
1 red eating apple, cored and chopped
2 hard-boiled eggs, chopped
50 g (2 oz) walnut halves, chopped
150 ml ($\frac{1}{4}$ pint) mayonnaise (see page 171)
15 ml (1 tbsp) lemon juice
freshly ground sea salt and pepper

Break the cauliflower into florets and wash well. Put all the ingredients in a salad bowl, season with salt and pepper and toss well together.

Serves 4

Petits pois à la française

25 g (1 oz) butter
1 small onion, skinned and chopped
6 lettuce leaves, washed and shredded
350 g (12 oz) shelled peas
freshly ground sea salt and pepper
5 ml (1 tsp) clear honey
chopped fresh parsley to garnish

Melt the butter in a saucepan, add the onion and cook for about 5 minutes until soft. Add the lettuce, peas, salt, pepper and honey. Cover and cook gently for 15–20 minutes, shaking the pan from time to time, until the peas are tender. Serve the peas hot, sprinkled with chopped parsley.

Serves 4

Grilled courgette and cheese slices

4 medium courgettes, trimmed
175 g (6 oz) Cheddar cheese, finely grated
10 ml (2 level tsp) grainy mustard
25 g (1 oz) walnuts, roughly chopped
freshly ground sea salt and pepper
15 ml (1 tbsp) Worcestershire sauce
15 g ($\frac{1}{2}$ oz) fresh wholemeal breadcrumbs

Blanch the courgettes in boiling salted water for 5–10 minutes until tender, then drain. Mix together the cheese, mustard, walnuts, seasoning and Worcestershire sauce. Cut the courgettes in half lengthways and spread half the cheese mixture over each. Sprinkle with wholemeal breadcrumbs and put under a pre-heated grill for 4–5 minutes, until crisp and brown. Serve hot.

Serves 4

Rainbow coleslaw

Illustrated in colour on page 178

225 g (8 oz) red cabbage
225 g (8 oz) white cabbage
1 large carrot, trimmed and scrubbed
$\frac{1}{2}$ a green pepper, seeded

For the dressing
150 ml ($\frac{1}{4}$ pint) soured cream
30 ml (2 level tbsp) mayonnaise (see page 171)
15 ml (1 tbsp) lemon juice
2.5 ml ($\frac{1}{2}$ level tsp) caraway seeds
2.5 ml ($\frac{1}{2}$ level tsp) celery salt
freshly ground sea salt and pepper

Trim and finely shred the red and white cabbages and put them in a large bowl. Grate the carrot on a coarse grater straight into the cabbage. Slice the green pepper finely and add it to the cabbage. Whisk the soured cream, mayonnaise, lemon juice, caraway seeds, celery salt, salt and pepper together until well blended. Pour this dressing over the coleslaw and mix thoroughly. Chill before serving.

Serves 4–6

Stir-fried mushrooms and bean sprouts

15 g ($\frac{1}{2}$ oz) butter
15 ml (1 tbsp) sunflower oil
1 medium onion, skinned and finely sliced
450 g (1 lb) mushrooms, wiped and sliced
225 g (8 oz) mung bean sprouts
freshly ground sea salt and pepper
grated rind and juice of $\frac{1}{2}$ an orange
25 g (1 oz) peanuts or cashew nuts

Heat the butter and oil in a large saucepan and fry the onion for 5 minutes until soft. Add the mushrooms and fry for a further 5 minutes until just tender. Stir in the bean sprouts, seasoning and orange rind and juice. Cook for a further 2–3 minutes, then spoon into a heated serving dish. Sprinkle with nuts and serve immediately.

Serves 4

Apricot and rice salad

225 g (8 oz) brown rice
100 g (4 oz) dried apricots, soaked overnight, drained and chopped
$\frac{1}{2}$ a medium red pepper, seeded and sliced
25 g (1 oz) flaked almonds, toasted
15 ml (1 level tbsp) chopped fresh chervil
freshly ground sea salt and pepper
45 ml (3 tbsp) French dressing (see page 172)
chopped fresh parsley to garnish

Put the rice into a saucepan and cover with salted water. Bring to the boil, cover and simmer for 40–45 minutes until the rice is just tender. Drain and rinse under cold running water to stop the cooking process, then drain again and leave to cool.

Stir the apricots, red pepper, almonds and chervil into the cold rice and season well. Pour the French dressing over the salad and toss well just before serving. Garnish with chopped parsley.

Serves 4

Italian pepper salad

Illustrated in colour on page 178

2 green peppers, seeded and sliced
2 red peppers, seeded and sliced
4 black olives, stoned and quartered

For the dressing
30 ml (2 tbsp) red wine vinegar
30 ml (2 tbsp) olive oil
5 ml (1 tsp) Worcestershire sauce
5 ml (1 level tsp) tomato purée
2.5 ml ($\frac{1}{2}$ level tsp) paprika
freshly ground sea salt
pinch of demerara sugar

Put the pepper slices in a pan of cold water, bring to the boil, then drain and cool.

Meanwhile, make the dressing. Put all the ingredients into a bowl and whisk well together. Arrange the cold peppers in a serving dish, pour over the dressing and leave for 30 minutes. Scatter the olives over the top. Serve as a side salad.

Serves 4

Vichy carrots

450 g (1 lb) new carrots, trimmed and scrubbed
400 ml ($\frac{3}{4}$ pint) cold water
25 g (1 oz) butter
freshly ground sea salt and pepper
5 ml (1 level tsp) demerara sugar
chopped fresh parsley to garnish

Place the carrots in a pan with the water, half the butter, a pinch of salt and the sugar. Bring to the boil and cook uncovered over a low heat, shaking occasionally towards the end, for about 45 minutes, until all the liquid has evaporated. Add the remaining butter and some freshly ground pepper and toss the carrots until glazed. Turn into a heated serving dish and sprinkle with parsley.

Serves 4

Turnip and watercress salad

350 g (12 oz) turnips, peeled
1 bunch of watercress, trimmed and washed

For the dressing
150 ml ($\frac{1}{4}$ pint) natural yogurt
10 ml (2 tsp) clear honey
5 ml (1 level tsp) mustard powder
15 ml (1 level tbsp) grated horseradish

Finely grate the turnips and chop the watercress and mix together in a salad bowl. To make the dressing, whisk the ingredients together until well blended, or put them in a screw-topped jar and shake vigorously. Stir into the salad. Leave the salad to stand for about 15 minutes before serving.

Serves 4

Tomato and onion salad

1 medium onion, skinned and sliced
freshly ground sea salt
3 large tomatoes, skinned and sliced
$\frac{1}{2}$ a medium green pepper, seeded and sliced
50 ml (2 fl oz) French dressing (see page 172)
chopped fresh parsley or basil to garnish

Sprinkle the onion slices with salt and leave to stand for 30 minutes. Rinse and drain well. Combine the onions, tomatoes and pepper, pour over the French dressing and toss well. Serve sprinkled with chopped parsley or basil.

Serves 2

Celery and alfalfa salad

1 small head of celery, trimmed and washed
100 g (4 oz) sprouted alfalfa
10 ml (2 level tsp) caraway seeds

For the dressing
60 ml (4 tbsp) soured cream
15 ml (1 tbsp) lemon juice
5 ml (1 tsp) clear honey
1 garlic clove, skinned and crushed
freshly ground sea salt and pepper

Finely chop the celery and put it in a salad bowl with the alfalfa sprouts and caraway seeds. To make the dressing, whisk all the ingredients together until well blended, or put them in a screw-topped jar and shake vigorously. Stir into the salad.

Serves 4

Savoy cabbage stuffed with mustard

2 very small Savoy cabbages
1 medium leek, trimmed and washed
45 ml (3 tbsp) olive or sunflower oil
10 ml (2 level tsp) mustard seeds
150 ml ($\frac{1}{4}$ pint) chicken stock

Cut each cabbage in half lengthways and scoop out the middles with a sharp knife, leaving four shells about 1 cm ($\frac{1}{2}$ inch) thick. Chop the cabbage middles and the leek very finely. Heat the oil in a flameproof casserole, large enough to take all the cabbage halves in one layer, and cook the chopped vegetables for about 10 minutes until they begin to soften. Stir in the mustard seeds and remove the pan from the heat.

Fill the cabbage shells with the cooked vegetables and pack them into the casserole. Return the casserole to the heat. Pour in the stock and bring to the boil. Cover the casserole and cook in the oven at 180°C (350°F) mark 4 for 45 minutes until tender.

Serves 4

Soured cream and mint dressing

150 ml ($\frac{1}{4}$ pint) soured cream
15 ml (1 level tbsp) finely chopped fresh mint
freshly ground sea salt and pepper
a little milk

Mix the soured cream and mint together and season to taste. Add enough milk to give the dressing a pouring consistency. Excellent with cold lamb cutlets.

Serves 4

Soured cream and watercress dressing

$\frac{1}{2}$ a bunch of watercress
150 ml ($\frac{1}{4}$ pint) soured cream
2.5 ml ($\frac{1}{2}$ tsp) lemon juice
freshly ground sea salt and pepper
a little milk

Remove the coarse stalks from the watercress and chop the rest finely. Mix with the soured cream and lemon juice and season to taste. Add enough milk to give a pouring consistency. This is an ideal dressing to serve with cold ham or cooked bacon.

Serves 4

NOTE This dressing is better made at least half an hour before serving.

Yogurt dressing

150 ml ($\frac{1}{4}$ pint) natural yogurt
1.25 ml ($\frac{1}{4}$ level tsp) mustard powder
freshly ground sea salt and pepper
15 ml (1 tbsp) lemon juice
15 ml (1 level tbsp) chopped fresh parsley

Place all the ingredients in a bowl and mix well together.

Makes 150 ml ($\frac{1}{4}$ pint)

Mayonnaise

1 egg
freshly ground sea salt and pepper
5 ml (1 level tsp) mustard powder
350 ml (12 fl oz) olive oil
45 ml (3 tbsp) white wine vinegar

Blend the egg, seasoning and mustard well together. Add the oil very gradually, beating constantly, or use an electric blender, until smooth and thick. Stir in the vinegar.

Makes 400 ml ($\frac{3}{4}$ pint)

Blender tomato dressing

30 ml (2 tbsp) tomato juice
30 ml (2 tbsp) cider vinegar
30 ml (2 tbsp) clear honey
1 egg yolk
30 ml (2 level tbsp) chopped fresh chives
1 sprig of parsley
60 ml (4 tbsp) sunflower oil

Put all the ingredients, except the oil, in a blender and blend for 30 seconds. Gradually add the sunflower oil and blend until smooth. This dressing is particularly suitable for a shredded cabbage salad.

Makes about 150 ml ($\frac{1}{4}$ pint)

French dressing

30 ml (2 tbsp) white wine vinegar or lemon juice
90 ml (6 tbsp) corn or sunflower oil
freshly ground sea salt and pepper
2.5 ml ($\frac{1}{2}$ level tsp) mustard powder
2.5 ml ($\frac{1}{2}$ level tsp) demerara sugar

Put all the ingredients in a bowl and whisk together until well blended. The oil separates out on standing so, if necessary, whisk the dressing again immediately before use. It is a good idea to store it in a bottle or screw-topped jar, shaking it up vigorously just before serving.

Makes 150 ml ($\frac{1}{4}$ pint)

NOTE The proportion of oil to vinegar can be varied according to taste. Use less oil if a sharper-flavoured dressing is preferred.

Soured cream and mushroom dressing

15 ml (1 tbsp) sunflower oil
15 ml (1 tbsp) lemon juice
freshly ground sea salt and pepper
25 g (1 oz) button mushrooms, wiped and finely chopped
150 ml ($\frac{1}{4}$ pint) soured cream
2.5 ml ($\frac{1}{2}$ level tsp) Worcestershire sauce
a little milk

Place the oil, lemon juice, salt and pepper in a bowl and mix thoroughly. Add the mushrooms and leave to marinate for 1 hour.

Drain off the excess oil and vinegar and mix the mushrooms with the soured cream and Worcestershire sauce. Adjust the seasoning. Add enough milk to give the dressing a pouring consistency. This dressing tastes good with seafood salads.

Serves 4

Soured cream and chive dressing

150 ml ($\frac{1}{4}$ pint) soured cream
15 ml (1 level tbsp) prepared mustard
15 ml (1 tbsp) white wine vinegar
30 ml (2 level tbsp) finely chopped fresh chives
freshly ground sea salt and pepper

Mix the soured cream, mustard, vinegar and chives together and season to taste. Use as a topping for baked jacket potatoes.

Serves 4

Soured cream and pickle dressing

150 ml ($\frac{1}{4}$ pint) soured cream
2.5 ml ($\frac{1}{2}$ level tsp) mustard pickle
freshly ground sea salt and pepper
a little milk

Mix the soured cream and mustard pickle together and season to taste. Add enough milk to give the dressing a pouring consistency. This dressing is delicious served with cold rare roast beef.

Serves 4

Sauces and Side Dishes

Although potatoes are the most popular accompaniment to most of our meals, the wholefood cook does not have to stick to them all the time as there are many whole grain products from which she can also take her pick to change the character of her meals. Bulgar, millet and kasha are becoming increasingly popular besides the now familiar brown rice and pasta. All these can be served with traditional British meals such as casseroles or with dishes of a more foreign flavour such as curry, goulash, a Bolognese-type sauce or a spicy pot of beans. Some, like millet and kasha can be made into croquettes and fried; and others such as bulgar, brown rice and pasta shapes can be mixed with salad dressings to accompany cold meats. They can be served quite plainly or mixed with vegetables in varying quantities; or they can become the basis of a main meal when meat, beans, cheese or chopped nuts are mixed in or cooked with them. All these whole grain products are particularly valuable for serving with secondary protein foods, so making a completely balanced meal.

Occasionally, you can treat plainer pulse dishes as an accompaniment instead of as a main dish. This more often applies to the light-coloured beans and peas such as butter beans, chick peas or haricot beans. Pease pudding is an example (see page 176) which is often used to accompany pork, and Dhal (see page 180) is a similar dish of lentils served with curries.

There is nothing wrong with occasionally serving bread with a meal, particularly if it is home-made and wholemeal; and with curries and other rich dishes serve Indian Puris (see page 180).

When a stuffing is called for, you need not discard your favourite recipe simply because it uses white breadcrumbs or white rice. Wholemeal crumbs and brown rice can easily be substituted and the stuffing will have a nutty flavour and be less stodgy (see page 181). Remember, though, that brown rice takes longer to cook than white so if the recipe calls for uncooked white rice it will be better to boil your brown rice for 20 minutes first. If you like bread sauce, wholemeal breadcrumbs can be used for that as well, again giving you a far superior flavour and texture to white (see page 185).

Most bought chutneys and sauces contain a high percentage of white sugar and some contain artificial colourings and flavourings. To make absolutely certain that you know what you are eating, have a go at making your own (see page 184). The flavour and colour will be perfectly natural and won't need to be improved upon. This way, not only your main dish, but all the extras and garnishes can be called wholefood as well.

Wholemeal noodles

Illustrated in colour on page 195

175 g (6 oz) plain wholemeal flour
1 egg
1 egg white
30 ml (2 tbsp) olive oil
5 ml (1 level tsp) freshly ground sea salt

Place the flour in a large mixing bowl. Make a well in the centre and add the remaining ingredients and 15 ml (1 tbsp) water. Mix together to form a soft dough. Knead the dough for 10 minutes on a lightly floured surface, until smooth and elastic, then re-flour the surface and roll out the dough to form a large paper-thin circle.

Lay the pasta on a clean dry cloth. Let one third of the pasta sheet hang over the side of the table and turn it every 10 minutes. This will help to dry the pasta more quickly. The drying process takes about 30 minutes and the pasta is ready to cut when it is dry and looks leathery.

Roll the pasta up loosely into a roll about 7.5 cm (3 inches) wide. Cut into 0.5-cm ($\frac{1}{4}$-inch) slices and leave for 10 minutes. To serve, cook in boiling salted water for about 8 minutes, until just tender.

Serving suggestions

Toss hot, drained noodles in butter then sprinkle generously with ground black pepper, chopped fresh herbs or grated Cheddar or Parmesan cheese. To serve as a main meal, chopped ham can be added or fry chopped onion or garlic in the butter before adding noodles. Alternatively, toss in a cheese sauce and sprinkle with parsley.

Makes about 350 g (12 oz)

NOTE Wholemeal noodles will keep for 2–3 days if covered and stored in the refrigerator.

Pease pudding

A traditional accompaniment to boiled ham or bacon.

225 g (8 oz) yellow split peas
freshly ground sea salt and pepper
1 ham bone or some bacon scraps
25 g (1 oz) butter or vegetable margarine
1 egg, beaten
pinch of demerara sugar

Rinse the peas and tie them loosely in a muslin cloth, place it in a saucepan with a pinch of salt, cover with boiling water and add the ham bone or bacon scraps. Boil for 2–2½ hours, or until the peas are soft.

Lift out the bag of peas and turn them into a sieve. Rub them through the sieve into a bowl and add the fat, egg, sugar and pepper to taste. Beat until thoroughly mixed, then tie up tightly in a floured cloth and boil for another 30 minutes. Turn on to a heated plate to serve. To give extra flavour, chopped onion or herbs may be added.

Serves 4

Curried millet

225 g (8 oz) millet
45 ml (3 level tbsp) mango chutney
25 g (1 oz) desiccated coconut, toasted
25 g (1 oz) seedless raisins
10 ml (2 level tsp) curry powder
2 bananas, peeled
juice of ½ a lemon
2 oranges

Cook the millet in 600 ml (1 pint) boiling salted water for 30 minutes until the water has been absorbed, then drain well. Mix in the mango chutney, and add the coconut, raisins and curry powder. Thinly slice the bananas, toss them in lemon juice and add to the millet. Peel and segment the oranges, stirring any juice into the mixture. Pile the millet mixture into a serving dish and arrange the orange segments down the centre. Serve as an accompaniment to a hot casserole.

Serves 6–8

Clockwise from top: Jerusalem artichoke and carrot purée (*page 165*),
Crunchy salad (*page 161*), Ratatouille (*page 163*)

Bulgar and grape salad

175 g (6 oz) bulgar wheat
2 sticks of celery, trimmed, washed and sliced
25 g (1 oz) currants
75 g (3 oz) black grapes, halved and pipped
40 g (1½ oz) whole almonds, toasted

For the dressing
45 ml (3 tbsp) sunflower oil
15 ml (1 tbsp) white wine vinegar
freshly ground sea salt and pepper
1.25 ml (¼ level tsp) mustard powder
grated rind and juice of ½ a small lemon
15 ml (1 tbsp) tahini paste

Soak the bulgar in cold water for 30 minutes, then drain and squeeze it dry. Mix the bulgar, celery, currants, grape halves and almonds together. Whisk the dressing ingredients together until well blended and pour over the bulgar mixture. Mix well and serve in individual bowls as an accompaniment to a savoury flan.

Serves 4

Crisp pasta salad

100 g (4 oz) wholewheat pasta rings, cooked
75 g (3 oz) red cabbage, trimmed and finely shredded
2 sticks of celery, trimmed, washed and finely sliced
50 g (2 oz) button mushrooms, wiped and sliced
1 leek, trimmed, washed and finely sliced

For the dressing
45 ml (3 tbsp) sunflower oil
15 ml (1 tbsp) red wine vinegar
15 ml (1 tbsp) Worcestershire sauce
15 ml (1 level tbsp) tomato purée
freshly ground sea salt and pepper
15 g (½ oz) sunflower seeds

Mix the pasta and vegetables together in a large bowl. Whisk the dressing ingredients together until well blended and pour over the pasta and vegetables. Mix well and pile into a serving dish. This makes a nice accompaniment to cold lean meats.

Serves 6

Clockwise from top: Tossed fresh spinach salad (*page 157*), Italian pepper salad (*page 168*), Minted cucumber and celery (*page 164*), Rainbow coleslaw (*page 167*), Apple, raisin and walnut salad (*page 163*)

Dhal (lentil purée)

100 g (4 oz) red lentils
300 ml (½ pint) cold water
30 ml (2 tbsp) sunflower oil
1 medium onion, skinned and finely chopped
25 g (1 oz) butter
freshly ground sea salt and pepper

There is no need to soak the lentils. Rinse them and put them in a pan with the cold water. Bring to the boil and simmer steadily for about 1 hour until tender, adding more water if they get too dry. Meanwhile, heat the oil in a pan and fry the onion for 5 minutes until soft.

When the lentils are tender, remove them from the heat and stir vigorously to form a purée. Add the butter and the fried onion and stir over the heat to blend well. Season with salt and pepper. Serve with curry.

Serves 4

Puris (Indian wafers)

100 g (4 oz) plain wholemeal flour
15 g (½ oz) butter or vegetable margarine
freshly ground sea salt and pepper
about 60 ml (4 tbsp) water
sunflower oil for frying

Put the flour in a bowl and rub in the fat. Season with salt and pepper. Gradually work in just enough water to give a pliable dough and knead well. If time permits, cover and leave the dough for 1 hour.

Roll out the dough wafer-thin between sheets of non-stick (silicone) paper, then cut out rounds about 8 cm (3 inches) in diameter. If they are not to be fried at once, cover the rounds lightly with a damp cloth until required.

Heat the oil in a frying pan and fry the rounds one or two at a time. Slide each raw puri into the oil and hold it down with a slotted spatula, pressing lightly to distribute the air. This produces the characteristic puffy appearance. Turn the puris once, remove carefully, drain on absorbent kitchen paper and serve as an accompaniment to a curry.

Makes 8

Sprouted wheat with herbs

60 ml (4 tbsp) olive or sunflower oil
1 medium onion, skinned and thinly sliced
1 garlic clove, skinned and finely chopped
225 g (8 oz) sprouted wheat
60 ml (4 level tbsp) chopped mixed fresh herbs

Heat the oil in a saucepan. Add the onion and garlic and cook for about 5 minutes until soft. Stir in the wheat and herbs and continue stirring for about 2 minutes, so that the wheat just heats through. Serve with lean cold meats.

Serves 4

Rice with peas

45 ml (3 tbsp) olive or sunflower oil
1 large onion, skinned and sliced
225 g (8 oz) brown rice
600 ml (1 pint) vegetable stock or water
450 g (1 lb) shelled peas
freshly ground sea salt and pepper
chopped fresh parsley to garnish

Heat the oil in a saucepan. Add the onion and cook for about 10 minutes, until lightly browned. Add the rice and cook for 2–3 minutes, stirring. Add the stock or water and bring to the boil. Reduce the heat and simmer, covered, for 40–45 minutes, until the rice is just tender, adding more liquid if necessary.

Cook the peas in boiling salted water for 10–12 minutes, until tender. Drain and stir into the cooked rice. Season well, sprinkle with chopped parsley and serve as an accompaniment to a hot casserole.

Serves 4

Rice stuffing

50 g (2 oz) brown rice, cooked
2 chicken livers, chopped
1 small onion, skinned and chopped
50 g (2 oz) seedless raisins
50 g (2 oz) blanched almonds, chopped
30 ml (2 level tbsp) chopped fresh parsley
25 g (1 oz) butter, melted
freshly ground sea salt and pepper
1 egg, beaten

Mix all the ingredients together, binding them well with the egg. Use as required.

Makes enough to stuff one 2-kg (4-lb) chicken, one 1-kg (2-lb) marrow or a large fish.

Kasha savoury

225 g (8 oz) buckwheat
50 g (2 oz) butter or vegetable margarine
1 medium onion, skinned and chopped
100 g (4 oz) mushrooms, wiped and sliced
freshly ground sea salt and pepper
600 ml (1 pint) chicken stock
4 large tomatoes, sliced
75 g (3 oz) Cheddar cheese, grated
chopped fresh parsley to garnish

Place the buckwheat in a large saucepan and heat gently for about 5 minutes until lightly toasted, shaking the pan continuously to prevent burning. Remove the buckwheat from the pan.

Heat the fat in the pan and fry the onion for 5 minutes until soft. Add the mushrooms and fry for a further 5 minutes. Stir in the buckwheat, seasoning and stock. Cover and simmer for 5 minutes or until the liquid has been absorbed. Spoon half the mixture into a shallow serving dish and cover with a layer of tomato and a layer of cheese. Top with the remaining buckwheat mixture. Sprinkle with more cheese and parsley and serve with lean cold pork.

Serves 6

Sprouted wheat salad

225 g (8 oz) sprouted wheat
1 small onion, skinned and finely chopped
50 g (2 oz) button mushrooms, wiped and thinly sliced
1 red pepper, seeded and finely chopped
6 black olives, stoned and quartered
30 ml (2 level tbsp) chopped fresh parsley

For the dressing
60 ml (4 tbsp) olive oil
30 ml (2 tbsp) white wine vinegar
freshly ground black pepper

Put the wheat into a bowl with the onion, mushrooms, pepper, olives and parsley. Whisk the dressing ingredients together until well blended. Stir this dressing into the salad and leave to stand for 15 minutes before serving.

Serves 4

Bulgar wheat and vegetable savoury

175 g (6 oz) bulgar wheat
400 ml ($\frac{3}{4}$ pint) boiling water
5 ml (1 level tsp) yeast extract
15 ml (1 tbsp) sunflower oil
1 medium onion, skinned and sliced
1 stick of celery, trimmed, washed and finely chopped
1 carrot, trimmed, scrubbed and finely sliced
1 leek, trimmed, washed and finely sliced
freshly ground sea salt and pepper
30 ml (2 level tbsp) chopped fresh parsley
2 tomatoes, skinned and chopped
2.5 ml ($\frac{1}{2}$ level tsp) paprika

Cook the bulgar wheat in the water with the yeast extract for about 10 minutes, or until all the liquid has been absorbed.

Heat the oil in a large saucepan and sauté the onion, celery, carrot and leek for 10 minutes until lightly browned. Stir in the bulgar wheat, season well and add 15 ml (1 level tbsp) of chopped parsley, the tomatoes and paprika. Serve in individual bowls, sprinkled with the remaining chopped parsley, as a side dish with lamb cutlets.

Serves 4

Brazilian stuffing

30 ml (2 tbsp) olive oil
1 small onion, skinned and chopped
1 small garlic clove, skinned and finely chopped
$\frac{1}{2}$ a green pepper, seeded and chopped
2 tomatoes, skinned and chopped
25 g (1 oz) sultanas
4 olives, stoned and sliced
50 g (2 oz) brown rice, cooked
freshly ground sea salt and pepper

Heat the oil in a frying pan, add the onion and cook for 3–4 minutes, until soft. Add the remaining ingredients and cook for about 10 minutes until they pulp slightly together. Use as required.

Makes enough to stuff one 1.5-kg (3-lb) chicken or a boned loin of pork.

Barbecued baked beans

1.1 litres (2 pints) tomato juice
1 large onion, skinned and chopped
60 ml (4 tbsp) cider vinegar
15 ml (1 tbsp) Worcestershire sauce
15 ml (1 level tbsp) mustard powder
15 ml (1 tbsp) molasses
freshly ground sea salt and pepper
5 ml (1 level tsp) paprika
350 g (12 oz) soaked and cooked haricot beans (see page 23)

Put all the ingredients, except the beans, in a large saucepan. Bring to the boil and cook rapidly until reduced by half, stirring from time to time. Leave to cool, then rub through a sieve or purée in a blender until smooth. Return to the pan, add the beans and simmer for 10–15 minutes.

Serve as an accompaniment to lean cooked meats or on hot, lightly buttered, wholemeal toast. Alternatively, serve with a salad as a main meal.

Serves 6

Mixed fruit chutney

450 g (1 lb) dried apricots, washed and roughly chopped
450 g (1 lb) stoned dates, roughly chopped
700 g (1½ lb) cooking apples, peeled, cored and chopped
450 g (1 lb) bananas, peeled and sliced
225 g (8 oz) onions, skinned and finely chopped
450 g (1 lb) Barbados sugar
grated rind and juice of 1 lemon
10 ml (2 level tsp) ground mixed spice
10 ml (2 level tsp) ground ginger
10 ml (2 level tsp) curry powder
10 ml (2 level tsp) freshly ground sea salt
900 ml (1½ pints) cider vinegar

Place all the ingredients in a large preserving pan. Stir over a low heat until the sugar has dissolved. Bring to the boil, then reduce the heat and simmer for about 1 hour, until thick and pulpy. Stir occasionally to prevent it sticking. Spoon into jars and cover. This chutney will keep for up to a year if stored in a cool, dry place.

Makes 3.2 kg (7 lb)

Tomato sauce

Illustrated in colour on page 52

50 g (2 oz) butter or vegetable margarine
450 g (1 lb) onions, skinned and chopped
2 garlic cloves, skinned and chopped
1.8 kg (4 lb) tomatoes, skinned and roughly chopped
10 ml (2 level tsp) demerara sugar
60 ml (4 level tbsp) tomato purée
pinch of paprika
freshly ground sea salt and pepper

Melt the fat in a saucepan. Add the onion and cook for about 10 minutes until soft. Stir in the garlic, tomatoes, sugar, tomato purée, paprika and seasoning. Cook, covered, for about 15 minutes until the onion and tomatoes are soft.

Makes 2.3 litres (4 pints)

Wholemeal bread sauce

3 cloves
1 small onion, skinned
300 ml ($\frac{1}{2}$ pint) milk
$\frac{1}{2}$ a bay leaf
1 blade of mace
50 g (2 oz) wholemeal breadcrumbs
freshly ground sea salt and pepper
15 g ($\frac{1}{2}$ oz) butter

Push the cloves into the onion. Put the milk into a saucepan with the onion, bay leaf and mace and bring it gently to the boil. Remove from the heat and leave to stand for 15 minutes.

Strain the milk and return it to the pan with the breadcrumbs. Season the mixture and heat gently, stirring, until it boils. Beat in the butter and serve the sauce hot as an accompaniment to poultry.

Makes about 300 ml ($\frac{1}{2}$ pint)

Puddings
and Desserts

We all feel like something sweet sometimes and, although if you eat wholefood you are leaving aside white sugar and large amounts of double cream, you can make some really mouthwatering desserts with all the ingredients that you have available.

Fruit provides natural sweetness and for some family meals, particularly when you are a little short of time, you can simply put a well stocked fruit bowl on the table for everyone to help themselves. It can also be accompanied by a dish of diced cheese and some chewy dates or figs.

Fresh fruit salads always go down well and they, too, are easy to prepare. Choose a selection of fruits in season including, for special occasions, the more exotic fruits like pineapple and black grapes. Instead of a sugar syrup, stir in a little honey or fresh fruit juice and let the fruits stand for about an hour so they produce their own sweet liquid. Fruit can also be lightly cooked with honey or Barbados sugar and served plainly or

made into a filling for pies and crumbles. Sieved or puréed fruit can provide a base for something more special like a mousse.

Dried fruits can be mixed with fresh into fruit salads and, by adding them to the more sour fruits like cooking apples and rhubarb, you will be able to cut down on the amount of other sweetener that you use. Dried fruits alone can be soaked in fruit juice for about 12 hours and then eaten just as they are or simmered for a few minutes with a cinnamon stick or strip of lemon rind to make a hot fruit compote. Soaked dried fruit can also be puréed in a blender and eaten as a soft dessert, either alone or mixed with a little yogurt or soured cream.

Yogurt alone, flavoured simply with honey or not at all, makes a refreshing end to a meal. You can fold raw or cooked fresh or dried fruit into it; or make more complicated yogurt-based dishes such as mousses and tarts.

Curd cheese is another useful ingredient for making low fat sweets which taste far richer than they actually are. The classic Russian Easter dish called Pashka (see page 197) is a good example, and then of course there are the old English curd tarts.

Pies and flans can all be made with wholemeal flour and crumble toppings are delicious made with Barbados or demerara sugar, wholemeal flour, wheatgerm and oatflakes. You can even make steamed brown puddings following any recipe for a white flour pudding.

Natural yogurt makes the best topping for all these sweet goodies. It has less fat and therefore less calories than cream and, besides that, its light flavour provides a pleasant contrast to anything rich and sweet. Custard, home-made with eggs and milk and with a little honey as a sweetener makes a hot alternative (see page 206).

A wholefood way of life can also be a sweet life.

Junket

This centuries-old sweet is made by adding rennet to milk. The rennet (which is prepared from the digestive juices of the calf) contains an enzyme that acts on the protein in milk and sets it, forming junket or 'curds and whey'.

568 ml (1 pint) milk
15–30 ml (1–2 level tbsp) demerara sugar
5 ml (1 tsp) liquid rennet
a little grated nutmeg

Gently heat the milk until just warm to the finger. Remove from the heat and stir in the sugar until dissolved. Add the rennet, stirring gently. Pour into a shallow dish and leave undisturbed until set. Sprinkle the top with a little grated nutmeg. In order not to kill the rennet enzyme, care must be taken not to overheat the milk, nor to cool the junket too rapidly. Junket should not be disturbed until it is served as once it is cut the whey runs out and separates from the curds.

Serves 4

NOTE Rennet is sold as a liquid or in a tablet without added colouring. There are also commercial preparations of rennet in powder, tablet and liquid form, which are already coloured and flavoured but these are not considered wholefood. Store rennet in a cool, dry place.

Osborne pudding

4 thin slices of wholemeal bread, lightly buttered
60 ml (4 tbsp) raw sugar marmalade
15 ml (1 level tbsp) demerara sugar
400 ml ($\frac{3}{4}$ pint) milk
2 eggs
a little grated nutmeg

Spread the bread and butter slices with marmalade. Cut into strips and arrange, marmalade side up, in layers in a greased ovenproof dish, sprinkling each layer with a little sugar.

Heat the milk, but do not allow it to boil. Lightly whisk the eggs and pour the milk on to them, stirring all the time. Pour the mixture over the bread, sprinkle some nutmeg on top and leave the pudding to stand for 15 minutes. Bake in the oven at 180°C (350°F) mark 4 for 30–40 minutes, until set and lightly browned.

Serves 4

Fresh orange and apricot muesli

50 g (2 oz) rolled oats
25 g (1 oz) seedless raisins
50 g (2 oz) dried apricots
150 ml ($\frac{1}{4}$ pint) milk
50 g (2 oz) wheatgerm
30 ml (2 level tbsp) demerara sugar
25 g (1 oz) hazelnuts, roughly chopped
3 large oranges
45 ml (3 tbsp) soured cream or natural yogurt
demerara sugar and hazelnuts to serve

Place the oats, raisins, apricots and milk in a bowl and leave to soak overnight.

The next day, stir in the wheatgerm, sugar and nuts. Add the juice of one orange and peel and segment the other two. Add to the muesli and stir in the soured cream or yogurt. Serve in individual bowls sprinkled with a little demerara sugar, if liked, and a few whole hazelnuts.

Serves 4